Spanish
Political Parties

Spanish
Political Parties

edited by

David Hanley
and John Loughlin

UNIVERSITY OF WALES PRESS
CARDIFF
2006

Published by the University of Wales Press

University of Wales Press
10 Columbus Walk
Brigantine Place
Cardiff
CF10 4UP

www.wales.ac.uk/press

Paperback   ISBN-10 0-7083-1931-9
            ISBN-13 978-0-7083-1931-4

Hardback   ISBN-10 0-7083-1831-2
            ISBN-13 978-0-7083-1831-7

British Library Cataloguing-in-Publication Data.
A catalogue record for this book is available from the British Library.

Printed in Great Britain by Antony Rowe Ltd, Wiltshire

Contents

Acknowledgements

This book has been long in the making and we would first of all like to thank the authors of the various chapters for their great patience in having to do several updates. We believe the result has been worth it. We would also like to thank Suzannah Lux, research assistant to John Loughlin, for her great diligence in helping to prepare the manuscript for publication. Andrew Dowling, our colleague in the School of European Studies, Cardiff University, kindly read parts of the manuscript.

Introduction

The Emergence of the Spanish Party System: historical background and contemporary realities

JOHN LOUGHLIN AND DAVID HANLEY

1. The historical background: regime changes in Spain

Spain has gone through many regime changes before settling down in the late twentieth century as a liberal-democratic state and full member of the European Union. Its geographical location as a peninsula in the south of Europe, separated by the Pyrenees mountains, meant, however, that, historically, it has been somewhat separate from the rest of Europe. Its cultural heritage is complex, with seven centuries of occupation by the Moors being followed by a long period of rule by Catholic monarchs in which the Church played a key role, both politically and in the sphere of culture.[1] It has had a distinct pattern of national development and was for long perceived as being distinct from the rest of Europe.

A further reason for this ambiguity in Spain's relations with the rest of Europe was its expansion beyond Europe. Its extensive coastlines on the Mediterranean and the Atlantic led it, soon after the conquest, to discover a maritime vocation, and the Spanish were heavily involved in the exploration of the New World, discovered by Christopher Columbus. Spain thus became the centre of an empire which covered most of South America (the exception being Brazil, a colony of Portugal which itself had broken away from Spain to become an independent state), all of Central America and part of North America (California, New Mexico and Florida were originally under Spanish rule).[2] The Spanish Empire was also involved in conquests of territory on the European continent, such as in the Low Countries, but its main focus was on the New World, which provided abundant resources of precious metals and raw materials. Furthermore, Spain's European conquests began to be reversed with the defeat of the Armada by England in the sixteenth century. The occupation by Napoleon at the beginning of the nineteenth century led to the loss of its American colonies which used the opportunity of the mother country's difficulties to declare independence. Military defeat by the US at the end of the nineteenth century meant the loss of Spain's remaining colonies in North America and the Philippines. By the early twentieth century, then, Spain, with the possible exception of Catalonia, was a rather isolated and inward-looking country separated by the mountains and the sea from the outside world.

This long and complex history implied a distinct pattern of political development for Spain with a number of regime changes throughout the nineteenth and twentieth centuries.[3] The period of Napoleonic rule (1808–14), although brief, was nevertheless of great importance in the subsequent evolution of the Spanish state, as it provided a centralized model of the state, based on the French Jacobin tradition,[4] that was an alternative both to the monarchy and to the decentralized, federal approach favoured by the national minorities such as the Basques and Catalans.[5] Throughout the nineteenth century, Spanish political life was dominated by the struggle between Carlists[6] and liberals with a brief period of the First Republic (1873 to 1875). In 1923, General Primo de Rivera established an authoritarian dictatorship.

The Primo de Rivera dictatorship was replaced in 1931 by the democratic regime of the Second Republic, a decentralized system with regional government in Catalonia (1932) and the Basque Country (1936) and an incipient one in Galicia which never materialized because of the outbreak of the Civil War. The Republic came to an end in 1939 after this war, which ensued when General Franco launched a revolt in 1936 against the Republic, in the name of the Spanish 'nation'.[7] The Civil War between nationalists and republicans could be seen as part of the wider conflict in Europe at that time, fought out among the three principal ideological forces: the extreme right (Nazis and fascists), Soviet communism, and liberal capitalism. Franco was supported by Hitler and Mussolini, while the Republicans received some support from the USSR (limited, conditional and channelled wherever possible to the Communist Party rather than to the Republic as a whole) and from at least some other Western states, particularly Mexico, with its republican and anti-clerical traditions. The main European democracies, France and Britain, stayed out of the war, thanks to the so-called Non-Intervention Pact of 1936, which meant that they ceased to help the legally elected government of Spain against a military coup. Germany and Italy, also signatories of the

Non-Intervention Pact, simply disregarded it and helped Franco massively with men and equipment. In many ways the Civil War was a trial run for the Second World War and allowed Hitler, in particular, to try out some of the new techniques of warfare as in the bombing of Guernica in the Basque Country, immortalized in Picasso's painting of that event. Within Spain, the Civil War claimed the lives of between 600,000 and a million Spaniards and foreigners (the debate about numbers continues) and left a legacy of great bitterness. Francoist Spain did not participate in the Second World War, but the victory of the Allies and Spain's previous association with the Axis powers meant that its isolation from the rest of Europe was intensified. The opposition to Francoism came from the left (mainly from the Spanish Communist Party and, to a lesser extent, from the Spanish Socialist Workers' Party) and from Catalonia and the Basque Country. The leadership of the opposition, however, mostly lived abroad. The dictatorship lasted until Franco's death in 1975. It was these events which dominate contemporary Spanish politics and the nature of Spanish political parties.

2. The Transition to Democracy post-Franco

It is remarkable that, given this highly-charged and dramatic history, the transition to democracy after Franco's death should have been so smooth.[8] This transition was far from a foregone conclusion. Many within Franco's entourage envisaged a continuation of the authoritarian regime and were opposed to liberal democracy. Franco himself had prepared Juan Carlos, the son of the Spanish king in exile, to succeed him in order to reinstate the monarchy, but a monarchy which would perpetuate the regime. In fact, Juan Carlos, although he had been groomed by Franco since he was a boy, had other ideas. He became personally convinced that the way forward for Spain was the democratic and European route. In this he was supported by a group of 'modernizers' within Franco's elites, especially a younger generation, who had not been directly involved in the Civil War. The Catholic lay organization, Opus Dei, despite its reputation for conservatism, played a key role in forming this new elite in a more technocratic and modernizing approach particularly in economic affairs. Among these new elites were Manuel Fraga, a Galician but at that time strongly in favour of the centralized state (he later converted to regionalism when he moved back to Galicia), and Adolfo Suárez, a younger Francoist who was also in favour of democratization. Behind the scenes, the Catholic hierarchy, who had traditionally supported Franco, now worked in favour of democratization. Although still contending with more reactionary forces among the old elites and especially the armed forces, these modernizers and the king succeeded in selling the idea of democratization to the non-elected *Cortes* which became the constituent assembly whose task was to draw up a new constitution.

The opposition forces were also important in the transition to democracy. The main opposition to Franco had come from the Spanish Communist Party, whose leaders, such as Santiago Carrillo, its secretary general and Dolores Ibárruri Gómez (*La Pasionaria*) had been the leading lights from their exile in the USSR, as well as from the Basque nationalist movement. The Basques also spawned a violent opposition movement in the form of *Euskadi Ta Askatasuna* (ETA), founded by a group of students in 1959. The socialist opposition was more muted, while the Catalans concentrated on fostering democracy and preserving their culture and language. During the 1960s, after the Second Vatican Council of the Catholic Church, many of the junior clergy supported the left-wing and nationalist movements. In the early 1970s, these tendencies were reinforced by the theology of liberation writings emanating from Latin America, as well as the *nouvelle théologie* from France.

When Franco died, the opposition movements overwhelmingly realized that this was an opportunity for the peaceful transition to democracy. A good example of this new attitude could be found in Santiago Carrillo, leader of the Communist Party. Even before Franco's death, the *Partido Comunista de España* (PCE) had struck a distance from Moscow and was among the first of the European communist parties to develop the theory of 'Euro-communism'. This was a moderate form of communism, which abandoned radical notions of Marxist orthodoxy, such as violent class struggle, the vanguard role of the party, the dictatorship of the proletariat and submission to the Soviet Union.[9] The Spanish Socialist Workers' Party (henceforth the Socialist Party), although still tied to Marxist rhetoric, had, under the leadership of Felipe González, also moderated its positions and finally abandoned all pretensions to socialist revolution by accepting the capitalist system, although some have argued that it was always reformist.[10] Finally, the Catalans, while still attached to *catalanisme*, also took the moderate route and decided to facilitate the transition. The problem was the Basques. The moderate *Partido Nacionalista Vasco* (Basque Nationalist Party–PNV) had serious reservations about whether the new constitution would sufficiently recognize their demands for national status, while ETA decided to continue the 'armed struggle'. Nevertheless, despite these difficulties, Francoists and anti-Francoists, with the king facilitating matters in the background, successfully negotiated a new constitution, which came into effect in 1978, thus setting up a liberal representative democracy.[11]

The larger context of this successful transition was the desire on the part of the majority of Spaniards to rejoin the family of western democratic nations, especially the increasingly successful European Community (EC). The democratization of Spain was a preparation for entry into Europe and, at the same time, the prospect of Europeanization was a powerful stimulus towards democracy. Most Spaniards at the time of Franco's death were very keen to reconnect with the rest of Europe and wished to put the past behind them. This desire to look forward to the future had important implications for the nature of the transition itself. First of all, parties or groups which were strongly identified with the Francoist period, either as supporters of Franco or, indeed, as his fiercest opponents, were penalized in the early period of transition. An example of this was the failure of the attempted military coup in 1981, when Lieutenant Colonel Antonio Tejero, an officer of the Civil Guard, invaded the *Cortes*, brandishing a pistol. The coup was quickly quelled and, in fact, helped to consolidate the transition by swinging public opinion firmly behind it. Other figures identified with the Franco period also failed at the national level. An example was Manuel Fraga, the founder of the *Alianza Popular* (AP), which later became the *Partido Popular* (PP). Although mostly favourable to the transition, Fraga was forced by his previous close association with Franco to abandon the leadership of the party at the national level and, in the late 1980s, to retreat to his home region of Galicia (from which Franco also originated) and build up a power base there. On the left, also, too close an association with the past could be an obstacle to success in the new Spain. The Communist Party had been in the forefront of the resistance to Franco and might have expected, as heroes of the resistance, to pick up advantages after the transition. In practice, the opposite happened, as the party did poorly in the polls and in time it almost went out of existence. It survived in the end, thanks to its joining and leading a coalition of left-wing groups called *Izquierda Unida* (IU–United Left). Commentators have suggested that the main reason for the party's decline was its association with the past rather than the future. This was also the main reason why the Socialist Party, under the leadership of Felipe González, had to reinvent itself by abandoning its Marxist rhetoric and adopting a more moderate social-democratic approach. Even the relative youth and photogenic features of both González on the left and Suárez on the right were important in presenting a modern image of the new Spain, the message being that the old, divided and bitter Spain of the Civil War and Franco dictatorship was being left behind. This was the message most Spaniards wished to hear.

In the end, the principal groups of left and right arrived at a consensus that a moderate approach to democracy and to the inclusion of Spain in the European family of nations was necessary. The extremes of right and left, those who wished to preserve the status quo of Francoism and those who wished to usher in socialist revolution, were relegated to the margins of the political scene. It is sometimes remarked that '*la transición fue una transacción*' (the transition was a transaction) in the sense that the two main blocs of right and left entered a series of pacts with each other, an approach that has been called 'pactism'. The communist leader, Santiago Carrillo, called the transition '*una ruptura pactada*', a breach with the past on the basis of consensus.

3. The Spanish Constitution and the Transition to Democracy

Another important aspect of this forward- and outward-looking dimension of the transition was the link made between Europeanization, democratization and decentralization. Francoist Spain had been isolationist, authoritarian and highly centralized, repressive of Spain's linguistic and national minorities. The new Spain would be European, democratic and decentralized. The Spanish constitution, drawn up by representatives of the main groups and approved by the *Cortes* in December 1978, reflects these aspirations and compromises. The aspirations are contained in the constitutional grounding of the principles of democracy, pluralism, free elections and the various freedoms and rights associated with liberal democracy. The constitution also endorses the principle of decentralization but it is here that ambiguities arose. The principal ambiguity concerns the way in which the constitution defines Spain as a nation. Article 2 states that: 'The constitution is based on the indissoluble unity of the Spanish Nation, the common and indivisible country of all Spaniards; it recognizes and guarantees the right to autonomy of the nationalities and regions of which it is composed, and solidarity amongst them all.' Thus, the Spanish nation is 'common and indivisible' and includes *all* Spaniards, meaning Basques, Catalans and Galicians as well as those of the other regions. On the other hand, there are also 'nationalities and regions'. The principle of political decentralization or autonomy was granted in this same article thus making Spain into an 'autonomic state' or, as it is put in Spanish, an '*Estado de las Autonomías*' (state of the autonomies). But the full working out and institutional expression of this principle was left to future practical politics. These ambiguities reflect the contradictions and tensions of Spain's history of state formation: on the one hand, the Napoleonic heritage of centralization; on the other, the existence of distinct national minorities. There are thus two, contradictory, tendencies at work in the constitution, centralization and decentralization, which have still not been satisfactorily reconciled.

Most politicians and citizens probably understood implicitly that the 'nationalities' in the Constitution referred to Catalonia, the Basque Country and Galicia, each of which has a distinct language and history and had enjoyed (at least in the first two cases) distinctive political and administrative institutions in the past. The 'regions' were those territories who wished to have their own regional governments, also known as Autonomous Communities (ACs). To some extent, the model for this distinction between 'special' and 'ordinary' regions was the Italian constitution of 1948, which had created five special and fifteen ordinary regions. In the end, all of the regions, even very artificial ones such as Madrid or La Rioja, opted in referendums to become ACs, although the conditions for acceding to this status differed between the two groups. The three 'nationalities' or 'stateless nations', as well as Andalusia could attain fully-fledged AC status, immediately following their referendums. The ordinary regions, however, could obtain full status only after five years. This distinction between different kinds of regions and/or nationalities has been a subject of political controversy since the transition to democracy. The right, and in particular the PP, but also some socialists, have been unhappy with differentiating parts of the territory in this way as they emphasize the 'unity and indivisibility' of the nation-state. Minority nationalists, however, have been very keen to maintain the differences.

Some aspects of decentralization, particularly the fiscal aspects (that is, giving fiscal autonomy to the ACs), were postponed to the future and implemented only in a piecemeal way over a long period of time. In effect, what has happened is that no-one is completely satisfied with the 'autonomization' process and these practical arrangements have introduced a dynamic into the process that has made it difficult to achieve stability. The three stateless nations strive continuously to maintain their difference from the 'ordinary' regions, while the latter have tried, largely successfully, to 'catch up' with the more advanced group. All the regions and nationalities have been unhappy with the fiscal arrangements as these meant, in effect, continuing fiscal centralization giving Madrid a power at odds with the political arrangements, although in recent years this has been largely rectified.[12] Sometimes, during periods of hung parliaments at the national level, when either the socialists or the PP formed minority governments, the latter entered into pacts with the moderate Catalan *Convergència i Unió* (CiU) or the PNV, parties represented in the *Cortes*, who managed to wring some concessions from them especially on the question of fiscal decentralization.

The final cause of tension resulting from the new constitutional arrangements has been the continuing sore of political violence in the Basque Country.[13] The majority of Catalan parties, whether nationalist or socialist, all of whom are catalanist (that is, promoting the Catalan language and culture), accepted the 1978 constitution and, basically, came to terms with being part of the Spanish state provided they had a large amount of political autonomy and their language and culture were preserved. Indeed, Jordi Pujol, the leader of the CiU and president of the *Generalitat* until 2003, was an expert politician having been elected a Deputy in 1977 and successfully operating on the Catalan, Spanish and European stages at the same time. Only the Catalan Republican Left espoused the goal of independence and even they eschewed violence to obtain that end. The Basque Country was very different. Both moderate (PNV) and radical (ETA and *Herri Batasuna*, HB) nationalists were critical of the constitution, which they felt did not adequately reflect Basque aspirations to national sovereignty. Although the moderate nationalists of the PNV rejected violence and agreed to work within the new system but with a view to changing the Constitution, ETA continued and even intensified its campaign of violence throughout the period of transition. The PNV has been the dominant party in the Basque Country and, in practice, accepted the system, but they are continually outflanked by the radical nationalists and must maintain a more critical distance from the centre in Madrid than their Catalan counterparts in the CiU. Galicia has been dominated since 1988 by the right-wing PP led by Manuel Fraga, who has turned this region almost into a personal fiefdom. Fraga has converted from the Jacobin centralism of his Francoist younger days to a kind of moderate regionalism. On his left, however, is the growing nationalist movement, the *Bloque Nacionalista Galego* (BNG), which, in coalition with the Galician socialists, ousted Fraga and the PP from power in June 2005.

4. The Main Cleavages in the Spanish Political System

The above brief outline of the history and the 1978 constitution display what are, in party political terms, the main cleavages of the Spanish political system. In any modern society, as universal suffrage is introduced and democratic ways of conducting politics develop, a number of fault-lines within the society become apparent. These cleavages, as political science vocabulary terms them, arise around major issues surrounding the development of the society in question, and society tends to divide on either side of the cleavage. It is from these divisions of opinion that modern parties are formed. The cleavages in modern Spain are twofold: the left–right cleavage, and the territorial one. The third great cleavage, between Church and State, which has figured hugely in Mediterranean Europe, has disappeared, or at any rate exists only in muted form in Spain (although it has made a comeback with the election in 2004 of the Socialist Party, which has launched a series of measures which have greatly irritated the Church, including legalizing homosexual marriages with adoption rights, liberalizing abortion and cutting down religious education in schools). What happened typically across Southern Europe was that liberal regimes based on rationalism, individualism and anti-clericalism, attacked the Church's positions in public life, attempting to end its control of any part of the education system or, in some cases, to take over its assets. The Church hierarchy usually responded by mobilizing Catholics, at first in civic associations, then increasingly in Catholic parties, which progressively became what we today call Christian Democrat (parties concerned to defend the Catholic religion by winning over voters on the basis of a social doctrine that stresses the common good). Such was the turbulence of political life in Spain, however, that there was never really a long enough democratic interlude for this type of party politics – liberals vs. Christian democrats – to take place.

By the end of the Franco dictatorship, the classic demands of liberal parties (personal freedoms based on a rationalistic concept of the individual) were carried adequately by the *Partido Socialista Obrero Español* (PSOE) or the *Izquierda Unida*, obviating the need for a traditional type of liberal party. Equally, on the Catholic side, the hierarchy saw no need to set up a specifically Christian party (particularly as Christian democracy was even then beginning to lose its political influence across Europe), thinking that Catholic interests could be adequately defended in a broad-based conservative party, as the PP was to become. So the main cleavages in Spanish society remain those between capital and labour, and centre and periphery. It is these which find their expression in the different political parties treated in this volume.

The left–right cleavage refers to the classic one between labour and capital or between workers and capitalists. Politically, the cleavage expressed itself through the formation of socialist and communist parties on the one hand and conservative and liberal parties on the other. This, however, is a rather simplistic expression of what is, in fact, a very complex phenomenon. There are different brands of socialism and, indeed, of communism. In the Spanish case, both the PSOE and the PCE emanated from the same Marxist family and the split between the two reflected the splits in the international socialist movement, the Second International, which occurred following the success of the Bolsheviks in the Russian Revolution in 1917. This spawned communist parties, united in the Third International, in other countries; these parties were more or less modelled on the Soviet party and were obedient to Moscow. Doctrinaire communism of this variety preached a set of political dogmas, such as the historical necessity of violent revolution, class struggle, the vanguard role of the party and the dictatorship of the proletariat. Bourgeois liberal democracy was denounced. The socialists, who retained control of the Second International, more or less abandoned these dogmas and, accepting the institutions of liberal democracy, sought to obtain the objective of a socialist state through democratic means. In practice, the Second International contained parties as diverse as the British Labour Party, the German Social Democratic Party (SPD) and the Spanish PSOE, all with quite distinct characteristics. In Spain, there were also movements to the left of the PCE and PSOE, such as the anarcho-syndicalists who achieved a remarkable strength in some regions such as Catalonia from the end of the nineteenth century to the time of the Civil War.

Franco's victory in the Civil War drove the left underground but it continued to exist as the representative of the working classes, although the anarcho-syndicalists faded out of existence. The extreme right was already represented in Franco's Falangist Party, although it is doubtful whether the party as a whole could be equated with Hitler's Nazis or even with Mussolini's Fascists. It was, rather, a conservative and authoritarian party, which espoused nationalism but without the racialist overtones of the Nazis.

The left–right cleavage is still important in contemporary Spain but expresses itself in much less stark terms than in the earlier periods. National politics is dominated by two large political 'blocs', led by the PSOE and the PP, but these are now centre-left and centre-right and, in many respects, there is arguably little to choose between them with regard to their policies except for individual rights and welfare. The PSOE, like the German SPD or the British Labour Party, accepts the capitalist economic system and 'bourgeois' liberal democracy, while the PP has long since abandoned the authoritarian features of Franco-ism and is even sympathetic to milder forms of social welfare. Indeed, it is striking that both the socialist Felipe González and the former PP leader José María Aznar strongly resemble the British prime minister, Tony Blair, and González anticipated many aspects of Blair's Third Way. This centrist orientation of the two parties harmonizes well with the mood of the country and the extremes of both right and left are relegated to the political wilderness. As has been the case across most of the developed world, left-wing groups have switched their emphasis away from the big questions of economic and social revolution or transformation, concentrating instead on themes which they feel are closer to today's voters. These include such issues as gender, environ-mental questions and individual rights in all fields. 'Choice' is often a keyword in this kind of political discourse which, historically, was long used by the liberal family of political parties before making its way on to the agenda of the (formerly) socialist left.

This downwards revision of political ambition by the left (and also by the right) is perhaps one explanation as to why there has been a smooth alternation between left and right: the early period of centre-right rule under Suárez gave way to a rather long period of socialist rule under González, which, in turn, was succeeded by Aznar's centre-right government. All of this is remarkable in a country whose history is littered with violent conflict and polarization.

At the national level, then, Spain has come to resemble most other Western states in the left–right cleavage, which is perhaps diminishing in importance as a way of categorizing political groups. Of greater significance is the territorial cleavage. Spain remains a country of geographical contrasts which overlap with nationalist/linguistic/cultural cleavages. Basically, as in Italy, the economic dynamism of the country has been situated in the north, in the Basque Country and Catalonia, while the south has remained economically and socially 'backward'. Although the Basque Country has experienced severe economic difficulties with the decline of its heavy industries of coal and steel, which were the backbone of its economy, Catalonia has been more successful in exploiting new forms of technological production and is more linked into international trade networks.

The populations of both regions, at both elite and mass levels, consider themselves to be 'stateless nations' (rather than 'nationalities') and not simply part of the Spanish 'nation'. There is thus a tension between the centralizing and Jacobin tendencies of Madrid governments, whether socialist or PP,[14] and the decentralizing and, in the case of the Basques, separatist tendencies of the two 'nations without states'. This, however, is not the only territorial cleavage. There is also an economic cleavage between the north and the south and this cleavage manifests itself at both national and regional levels. At national level, there is a certain amount of resentment on the part of the Catalans and Basques, as the rich part of Spain, who feel they are carrying the more backward regions. This is similar to the resentment felt by northern Italians towards the Italian Mezzogiorno, which has been exploited by Umberto Bossi's Northern League movement. In Spain, this has meant that it has been difficult to arrive at a system of financial equalization across the regions as this is resisted by the northerners. There are also repercussions at regional level, at least in the two northern regions. In the Basque Country, the support base of the PSOE and the PP largely consists of non-Basque immigrants from other parts of Spain although there are also some local Basque supporters. This has caused some resentment among native Basque nationalists, who feel that the southerners are a 'foreign' element in the Basque Country. It is intensified by the difficulties in learning the Basque language which bears no relation to any other language, including Spanish. The same situation occurs in Catalonia, which also experienced a large amount of immigration from the south. These southern immigrants have traditionally formed the bedrock of the

Partit dels Socialistes de Catalunya (PSC – federated to the PSOE) and PP support, although today their political allegiances are more complex as many have espoused Catalanism. Their position with regard to the language is, however, very different from that of their counterparts in the Basque Country, in that Catalan is relatively easily understood and learned by a Castilian (Spanish) speaker.[15] These difficulties have not arisen in Galicia, which has been less developed economically than the other two nationalities and has, therefore, not attracted a large non-Galician immigrant population. Furthermore, Galicia was more supportive of both Franco and the post-Franco PP, with Fraga as the local leader, and less prone to radical nationalism.

5. The Spanish Party Systems

Most contemporary studies of parties explore not just the various parties operating in any state at a given time, but the relationships between these actors. The sum total of these relationships is what is meant by the term 'party system'. Analysts used to classify party systems simply in terms of the number of parties (thus the UK was a two-party system, Canada a two-and-a-half party system, and so on). Today, however, following the work of scholars like Sartori,[16] more stress is placed on the nature of relations among the parties. Usually these are approached from the angle of party competition, but more subtle analyses often also look for patterns of complicity or collusion. There are some complex debates between various party system theorists, but for operative purposes we can simplify as follows.

The most frequently found types of system include that of bipolarization, where competition is between two main forces (other small parties may exist on the margins but be unable to reach government, as has long been the case with the UK Liberal Democrats); more often than not such parties are moderate. Multipolar systems, involving more than two parties with a realistic chance of being in government, can be either moderate or polarized (when one or more of the parties does not really accept the basic workings of the political institutions: classic examples are far-right parties and, during the Cold War at least, communist parties). One major ingredient in determining the nature of a party system is the electoral system. The more proportional the system, the more likely it is that several parties will win seats. The more it inclines to the UK system (only one ballot and first-past-the-post or winner-takes-all), the more likely it is that two big parties will emerge to contest the lion's share of the seats.

Like most states which combine a clearly delineated central government with strong subnational institutions endowed with varying degrees of power, Spain has not one party system, but several. (The UK, long considered the archetype of a centralized state with a rigid party system, is now beginning to experience the differentiation of the statewide party system from the new, regional party systems that are settling in within Wales and Scotland, as these territories consolidate their devolved regimes.) In Spain then, alongside a clearly recognizable statewide system of parties, there exists in every AC a regional party system, whose actors may well include statewide parties (or their regional branches, sometimes with different names from the Madrid party), as well as exclusively regional ones. Sometimes these two kinds of party can find themselves in different relationships, in Madrid and regionally, making for a very complex set of what we might call party subsystems.

The statewide party system is the easiest to understand, as it is clearly one of moderate bipolarism. Since the first democratic elections, the real choice for voters has lain between the PSOE (a moderate social democratic party) and a moderate conservative party, be it the *Unión de Centro Democrático* (UCD) or nowadays the PP (although this party, after its 2000 election victory, became less moderate). Conservative forces in Spain have managed to find sufficient unity between their different elements – those nostalgic for Francoism, market liberals or Christian democrats – to present themselves in one party. Yet at the same time, the element of proportionality in Spain's electoral system (deputies are elected to the lower house of the *Cortes* by a list system of PR in each province) does open the door for a certain amount of representation for smaller parties. The lower chamber which expired in March 2004, thus saw 78.7 per cent of its seats shared between the big two, PP and PSOE in 2000, with small numbers going to a third statewide force, the post-communist IU. The remaining thirty-four seats were scattered between no less than nine parties from the ACs, fifteen going to the Catalan CiU and seven to the Basque PNV. What this means is that in normal circumstances, governments can only be formed by PSOE or PP. If, as sometimes happens however, neither has a clear majority, then the smaller regional parties come into their own, or at least CiU and the PNV do. In recent years, both these formations have supported Madrid governments of PP or PSOE in return for policy concessions, despite sometimes being in opposition to the Madrid governing party within their own AC. The only time they can exercise any influence, however, is in a 'hung parliament'. Otherwise, like their colleagues from the other regional parties, their role is largely one of flying the regional flag in Madrid and hoping to be more influential in the party system of their own ACs. UK readers will notice the similarity between this situation and that of the nationalist parties in Scotland and Wales, the Scottish National Party and Plaid Cymru.

Within the ACs, the situation of regionalist/nationalist parties can vary immensely. In both the Basque Country and, until 2003, Catalonia, the nationalist party was, in Sartori's terms, a dominant party, that is, it always took the biggest share of the seats (although the socialists won the highest percentage of votes in the 1999 elections) and would normally expect to form the government, with the other parties in the system having to base their actions on this assumption. In both these multiparty systems, local nationalist parties competed with statewide parties in suitable local guise, the result being a rather untidy scattering of seats among the two sorts of party (see chapters on the ACs). There is a major difference between the dynamics of the two systems, though, in that Catalonia can be described as having a moderate multi-party system, where even the anti-system party, the pro-independence *Esquerra Republicana de Catalunya* (ERC), accepts the rules of the electoral game. After the 2003 Catalan elections ERC even joined the PSC and the Greens to form a three-party ruling coalition. In the Basque Country, however, the multipartism is seriously polarized between a group of parties, nationalist and statewide, prepared to work within the constitution and a militant independentist party *Batasuna* (previously *Herri Batasuna*), now banned by the Madrid government, close to the ETA organization that wages a military campaign in pursuit of independence. As a result, *HB/Batasuna* has usually been unavailable as a potential coalition partner, thus obliging the PNV to look for allies among the statewide parties on occasion. This makes for a high degree of instability within the party system, as a significant part of the electorate (*Batasuna* voters and potential supporters) are effectively disenfranchized, either because their party is disregarded or, as recently happened, simply outlawed. The fate of the locally dominant parties has varied of late. The PNV still dominates Basque political life but the loss of control by the CiU late in 2003 to the PSC and allies threatened to open up a new phase of the Catalan party system.

Conclusions: a fully-fledged democratic state

The story of contemporary Spain is a remarkable one of transition from an undemocratic authoritarian state to a healthy and stable liberal democracy, having successfully weathered the crisis of an attempted *coup d'état* in 1981. The political parties, alongside other forces of Spanish society, such as the monarchy, the Catholic Church and the trade unions, have been essential actors in this transition and this is true, whether the parties are of the right or the left. There has, indeed, been an alternation of power by the two main national parties, the conservative PP and the centre-left socialists. Furthermore, at times, nationalist parties from Catalonia and the Basque Country have also participated in national political life, by holding the balance of power in hung elections. A strong feature of the Spanish political system is the coexistence of national and regional (AC) party systems, which makes the system quite complex. The national parties are present in all of the regions but in the Basque Country the dominant parties are the nationalists while in Catalonia the new government is based on a centre-left coalition including the separatist ERC. In Galicia, the previous dominant party, the conservative PP, dominated by Manuel Fraga, has been replaced by a coalition of the nationalist BNG and the socialists. There are small regionalist parties in the other regions but these, by and large, are dominated by the big national parties. European integration is the larger context, which has made possible this transition to democracy and almost all the parties are pro-European. This is not to say that there are no tensions. The 'autonomic process' is still not complete and there are, at times, tensions between Madrid and the ACs, especially in the cases of Catalonia and the Basques. Furthermore, the question of the relations between the Basque Country and the rest of Spain is still a sore point. Attempts to apply a Northern Ireland Agreement solution have failed abysmally, thanks to the intransigence of the Aznar government, as well as of ETA.[17] Now the PNV has turned to the Quebecois nationalist strategy of 'sovereignty association' as a possible solution. It is unlikely that this will have greater success than the Northern Ireland model. In the meantime, violence continues.

Plan of this book

The chapters of this book attempt to lay out the essential features of the two levels of party system. There are chapters on the two main national parties, the PSOE and the PP, as well as on those in the main Autonomous Communities.[18] Each of these chapters details something of the history of the party or parties concerned, their organization and support base, and how they have performed in recent elections. The purpose of the book is to stimulate further interest on the part of the student and, with this end in view, there is a bibliography at the end of each chapter for further reading.

The dramatic election of Sunday 14 March 2004 apparently presaged a major shift in Spanish politics. The previous Thursday, terrorist bombs planted in commuter trains at Madrid's Atocha station had killed over 200 people and wounded over a thousand. Spontaneous mass demonstrations of solidarity erupted all over Spain, bringing millions on to the streets. The government promptly blamed ETA, though that organization had never wrought destruction on such a scale or with such a mode of operation. Evidence soon pointed to the involvement of fundamentalist Islamist organizations, which the government seemed rather reluctant to acknowledge; it was even suggested (*Le Monde* 16 March 2004) that sources in the Spanish intelligence services, exasperated at the thought of an attempt to play electoral games with such a grave issue, had threatened to leak evidence to the press unless Aznar revealed what was known. Clearly, blaming ETA was likely to be productive in terms of increasing the centralist PP's vote, while Islamist involvement would have the opposite effect. If Spain had been hit in reprisal for its support for Bush and the Gulf war, then the 90 per cent of Spaniards who had opposed Spanish involvement in the war would have serious doubts about the wisdom of such an uncritically Atlanticist foreign policy. Aznar's apparent attempts to turn the Madrid rally into an election call for the PP (the main slogan on the banner spoke of loyalty to the constitution, a true centralizer's buzzword) was also insensitive.

In the end, voters punished the PP massively for the consequences of its policy and the way in which it had tried to evade them. A lead of five or six points in the polls days before the election was turned into a crushing defeat. Turnout increased by 8 per cent to 77.2 per cent, with many of the two million young first-time voters clearly voting for the left. With a record 10,909,687 votes to the PP's 9,617,556, the PSOE beat its rival by a clear 5 per cent (42.64 per cent to 37.64 per cent), the PP losing 700,000 votes. The defeat was evenly spread across Spain, but with particular emphasis in the historic nationalities, where, in addition to the local organizations of the PSOE, regionalist parties did well, nowhere better than in Catalonia where the left-nationalist ERC went from one deputy to eight. A few weeks before, Aznar had forced its leader in the new Catalan executive, Carod Rovira, to be dismissed for having negotiated privately with ETA.

In terms of seats, the new *Cortes* comprised (figures in brackets show gains or losses from 2000):

PSOE:	164	(+39)
PP:	148	(-35)
ERC:	8	(+7)
IU:	5	(-4)
CiU:	10	(-5)
PNV:	7	
Eusko Alkartasuna – EA:	1	
Bloque Nacionalista Galego – BNG:	2	(-1)
Coalición Canaria – CC:	4	

One seat each for moderate nationalists from Aragon and Navarre.

Source: El Pais, 15 March 2004.

The PSOE leader José Luis Rodríguez Zapatero would clearly be able to form a majority government with support from smaller parties, and the PP duly conceded defeat. There can be few instances of foreign events impacting so directly on the politics of a country. But this is undoubtedly what happened in March 2004 to propel Spanish party politics into a new phase.

Notes

[1]   Raymond Carr, Spain 1808–1975, 2nd Edition (Oxford: Clarendon, 1982); Richard Fletcher, Moorish Spain (London: Phoenix, 1994) [originally published by Weidenfeld & Nicolson, 1992].

[2]   John Lynch, *Spain, 1516–1598: from nation state to world empire* (Oxford, UK; Cambridge, Mass., USA: Blackwell, 1991).

[3]   Raymond Carr (ed), *Spain: a history* (Oxford: Oxford University Press, 2000).

[4]   A concept designating those who believe passionately that the central state is always more enlightened and progressive than any devolved administration, which should be kept to the minimum possible. At the high point of the French Revolution (1792–4), the Jacobins were the faction who won a violent power struggle over their decentralizing rivals, the Girondins.

[5] Michael Glover, *Legacy of glory: the Bonaparte kingdom of Spain, 1808–13* (London : Leo Cooper, 1972)

[6] Carlism, a right-wing political movement, was created in 1833. The group took its name from Don Carlos, the youngest brother of King Ferdinand VII (1784–1833) and would-be King Carlos V. Carlists were opposed to liberal secularism and economic and political modernism. As a result Carlism received considerable support from the Spanish Catholic Church.

[7] Raymond Carr, *The Spanish tragedy: the Civil War in perspective* (London: Phoenix Press, 2000); Frances Lannon, *The Spanish civil war, 1936-1939* (Oxford: Osprey, 2002); Paul Preston, *A Concise History of the Spanish Civil War* (London: Fontana, 1996).

[8] Teresa Lawlor and Mike Rigby (with José Amodia, Ana María Plymen, Manuel Pérez Yruela and Rafael Serrano del Rosal), *Contemporary Spain: essays and texts on politics, economics, education and employment, and society* (London and New York: Longman, 1998).

[9] Santiago Carrillo, *'Eurocommunism' and the State* (London: Lawrence and Wishart, 1978); Paolo Filo della Torre, Edward Mortimer, and Jonathan Story (eds), *Eurocommunism: Myth or Reality?* (Harmondsworth: Penguin, 1979); Howard Machin (ed.), *National Communism in Western Europe*, London: Methuen, 1983); Michael Waller and Meindert Fennema (eds), *Communist Parties in Western Europe: Decline or Adaptation* (Oxford: Blackwell, 1988).

[10] Paul Heywood, *The government and politics of Spain* (Basingstoke: Macmillan, 1995).

[11] Teresa Lawlor and Mike Rigby, *Contemporary Spain* (London and New York: Longman, 1998).

[12] Eliseo Aja, 'Spain: Nation, Nationalities, and Regions' in John Loughlin et al., *Subnational Democracy in the European Union: Challenges and Opportunities* (Oxford University Press, 1st edition 2001, paperback edition, 2004) pp. 229–55; J. Loughlin and S. Martin, "Subnational Finances in Spain: Lessons for the UK?", Office of the Deputy Prime Minister, April 2004. available at *www.local.odpm.gov.uk/finance/balance/bof22.pdf*.

[13] John Loughlin and Francisco Letamendia, 'Peace in the Basque Country and Corsica', *Irish Studies in International Affairs*, 11, November (2000), 147–62.

[14] It is true that the PP and PSOE have different approaches to the regional question, with the PP tending to favour a moderate regionalism while the PSOE is more open to federalism (see the chapters in this volume for the differences).

[15] Daniele Conversi, *The Basques, The Catalans and Spain: Alternative Routes to Nationalist Mobilization* (Nevada: University of Nevada Press, 2000).

[16] Giovanni Sartori, *Parties and party systems: a framework for analysis*, Cambridge: Cambridge University Press, 1976).

[17] John Loughlin, 'Redefining Minority Nationalisms in Western Europe: new Contexts for Political Solutions in Northern Ireland, the Basque Country and Corsica', in John Darby and Roger MacGinty (eds.), *Contemporary Peace Making: Conflict, violence and peace processes*, London: Palgrave-Macmillan, 2002. pp. 38–49

[18] The other left-wing formation, Izquierda Unida, which includes the Spanish Communist Party, has been progressively weakened and is covered mainly in this introduction and in the chapter on the Socialist Party.

1

The Partido Popular

JOHN GILMOUR

Historical background[1]

The origins of the *Partido Popular* (PP) date from the early 1970s
when Manuel Fraga Iribarne, who had been Franco's minister of
information and tourism from 1962 to 1969, attempted to launch a
centrist movement to prevent power remaining in the hands of hard-
line Francoists or being seized by the anti-Franco opposition. He maintained that only a movement of this type could provide the stable
basis for Spain's political development and avoid another bloody
confrontation between polarized extremes. Directing operations from
London where he had been sent as Spanish ambassador in October
1973, he set up *Gabinete de Orientación y Documentación S.A.* (GODSA)
as a discussion group to draw up a programme of democratic reform.
In March 1976, after being appointed as interior minister and deputy
prime minister for political affairs in the government of Carlos Arias
Navarro, he launched his own party, *Reforma Democrática*, hoping
that it would spearhead the transition to democracy that had now
begun. However, the following July, when Adolfo Suárez unexpectedly
succeeded Arias, Fraga refused to serve in the new administration and
teamed up with other former ministers of the Franco dictatorship in
September to form *Alianza Popular* (AP), which was much further to
the right than he had previously envisaged.

Meanwhile, Pío Cabanillas Gallas, who had worked under Fraga in
the 1960s and shared his reformist views, had also been politically
active, helping to establish *Federación de Estudios Independientes S.A.*
(FEDISA), another study group with which Fraga was associated. In
this, he collaborated closely with members of the Asociación Católica
Nacional de Propagandistas, who had written a regular column in the
Catholic daily *Ya* in 1973 under the pen-name *Tácito*, calling for

greater democratic freedoms than the Franco government was prepared to allow. In November 1976, he helped launch a party calling itself *Partido Popular*, which was intended to occupy the centre ground between the AP and the socialists, and over the following months encouraged other liberal, social democrat and Christian democrats to join them in setting up a loose coalition calling itself the Centro Democrático. In the run-up to the 1977 general election, Leopoldo Calvo Sotelo, a FEDISA member and minister for EEC affairs in the Suárez government, persuaded the CD leaders to accept Adolfo Suárez as their candidate for prime minister and register their alliance as the *Unión de Centro Democrático* (UCD).

The UCD and the AP vied with each other for the centre-right vote until 1982. The UCD became *the* party of the transition, victorious in both the 1977 and 1979 general elections, although it failed to win an overall majority. However, it split into warring factions and was wound up in February 1983 after a humiliating defeat in the October 1982 general election at the hands of the PSOE. After that, Suárez kept his own brand of centrism alive with his *Centro Democrático y Social* party (CDS), but with limited success, and it faded from the scene after Suárez retired from active politics in 1991. By contrast, the AP suffered two heavy defeats in 1977 (when it was perceived as being too Francoist) and in 1979 (when Fraga set up the *Coalición Democrática* in a desperate attempt to woo the centrist vote away from Suárez). However, at its 1979 congress, the AP was relaunched under Fraga's sole leadership. It subsequently attracted the UCD's Christian democrat wing (principally Oscar Alzaga's *Partido Demócrata Popular* – PDP, which had fallen out with Suárez over the divorce law, and became the main opposition group to the *Partido Socialista Obrero Español* (PSOE) after 1982. The alliance between the AP and the PDP, known as *Coalición Popular*, never functioned smoothly, particularly after the small *Unión Liberal* party joined them, and it broke up after the 1986 general election, having failed to reduce the socialist majority. Fraga resigned as the AP leader in December 1986 and was replaced by Antonio Hernández Mancha, a young Extremaduran who tried to revolutionize the party but could not curb its infighting. The supporters of Miguel Herrero, whom Mancha had beaten in the leadership contest, including José María Aznar, urged Fraga to make a comeback. In February 1989, Mancha was persuaded to step down, and Fraga, in collaboration with former UCD Christian democrat, Marcelino Oreja, and acting on the suggestion of the latter's nephew, Jaime Mayor

Oreja, reconstituted the AP as the PP to bring it in line with centre-right parties elsewhere in Europe.[2] However, Fraga only saw himself as *presidente interino* (temporary leader), having already decided to retire from the national scene and stand in the 1989 regional election in Galicia. So when Felipe González called an early general election for 29 October, Fraga proposed Aznar as the PP's challenger early in September. Following a respectable election performance, Aznar was confirmed as leader at the PP's 10th congress in Seville in April 1990.

Under Aznar's leadership, the PP was transformed into a tightly structured and unified party, which, despite having evolved from the AP, saw itself as the UCD's successor. A few weeks before the 1996 general election, with the polls indicating the likelihood of a PP victory, Aznar proudly declared to his supporters at their 12th congress: 'Este es el partido que yo quería' ('This is the party I was looking for'). As Luis Herrero states, never before had the PP had an indisputable leader, never before had it enjoyed such internal harmony, never had it been so moderate, and never had it been so close to power.[3] Aznar stepped down as leader in 2003, after having led the PP to power in 1996 and again in 2000. He nominated Mariano Rajoy as his replacement at the end of August 2003, well in advance of the 2004 general election. Rajoy was generally acknowledged to be a safe pair of hands, someone with considerable experience in the party and government who had collaborated loyally with Aznar since the party's relaunch in 1990.

Party structure

From 1989 to 2005, Fraga enjoyed an uninterrupted period of power in Galicia and became a pillar of strength in Spain's regional politics. At the same time, as the PP's founder leader, he occupies the place of honour at national party congresses, is still revered by many in the party as 'The Boss' or simply '*Don Manuel*', and his old office at party headquarters is left unoccupied – such is the moral authority which he continues to hold. At their 10th congress, when he handed the reins formally to Aznar, he warned delegates: 'Yo seré un disciplinado e incondicional militante de José María Aznar, y no voy a tolerar maniobras ni intrigas contra el nuevo líder' ('I shall be a disciplined and unconditional supporter of José María Aznar and I will tolerate neither machinations nor plots against the new leader').[4] In other words, he saw himself as loyal to Aznar, but also the one who would keep everyone else in line.

From 1990 until 2003, Aznar was the PP's undisputed leader, enjoying full powers as its national president but allowing the final decisions to be made by the party executive. In that time, there was little sign of the kind of infighting that had plagued the AP under Mancha and Fraga. Perhaps, as Luis Herrero observes, the party united around Aznar out of a common desire to win power.[5] However, Aznar secured his own position by rejecting Miguel Herrero's idea of a *dirección colegiada* (collective leadership) and dispensing with deputy leaders such as Marcelino Oreja and Isabel Tocino who might have been tempted to challenge him. He remained a 'hands-on' leader, attending meetings of the PP's executive whenever possible and setting the political agenda. His successor, Mariano Rajoy, who was regarded as being much less aggressive, seems to have succeeded in leading the party through the disappointment of election defeat in 2004 without reigniting internal party feuds. However, proof of the mark that Aznar's leadership has left on the party and the influence that he continues to hold is provided by his current position as Honorary President at the top of the party hierarchy.

Until 1999, the remainder of the PP's leadership consisted of a general secretary, a coordinator, and seven assistant general secretaries, each of whom was responsible for a specific area of activity, and they formed a close-knit team, which became the backbone of the PP government in 1996. Rodrigo Rato recalls that 'todos cenábamos una vez al mes, junto a nuestras esposas, y ahí se creó un entramado de afectos entre nosotros y, sobre todo, un espíritu de equipo que era lo que no había existido nunca en la dirección de AP' (We all used to have dinner together once a month accompanied by our wives, so we all became very close and developed a team spirit that had never existed before at the head of the AP).[6] However, at the 13th congress in January 1999, Francisco Alvarez Cascos, the PP's hardman (or bruiser) in the Fraga mould, was replaced as general secretary by Javier Arenas, a much more emollient centrist who, having stood down as minister of labour, was now free to concentrate on party affairs. Another significant change had occurred the previous July, when the aggressive Miguel Angel Rodríguez resigned as government and party spokesman. His duties were split between industry minister Josep Piqué and Rafael Hernando respectively, with Piqué giving way to Pío Cabanillas Alonso after becoming foreign affairs minister in

March 2000. Aznar also made Hernando 'communication' coordinator in his new leadership team in January 1999 alongside Pío García Escudero, Mercedes de la Merced and Ana Mato (as 'organization', 'induction' and 'participation' coordinators respectively), with Rodrigo Rato, Mariano Rajoy and Jaime Mayor Oreja remaining as the three assistant secretaries.[7] These changes introduced much younger faces into a softer and more streamlined party hierarchy. The assistant secretaries were widely regarded as the front runners for the PP leadership after Aznar. In fact two of them, Rajoy and Rato were appointed as deputy prime ministers in Aznar's new, expanded cabinet following the March 2000 elections. In September 2003, in line with Aznar's decision not to stand as party leader in the 2004 elections, the party executive approved his proposal to nominate Rajoy as his successor and new general secretary. Then, at the party's 15th Congress in October 2004, Rajoy was elected president, with Angel Acebes taking over as party secretary and creating a new team of six executive secretaries responsible for organization, communication, autonomy policy, social policy, economic policy and people's rights. PP's executive and its steering committee, the *Junta Directiva Nacional*, fulfil the same functions as they did within the old AP hierarchy. However, Aznar trimmed the executive by almost half, with an increase in the number of women (currently they outnumber the men by twenty-one to nineteen) and the reinforcement of representation from the Autonomous Communities, especially Catalonia. In the lower reaches of the party, few of the old Francoist guard remain. In 1993, seven new regional presidents and thirty-one provincial presidents were elected, even where the PP held power. Earlier that year changes were made to the party statutes, preventing the same person from holding the position of president or secretary at provincial or regional level as well as a parliamentary seat. A member of the PP executive remarked: 'El presidente provincial del partido lo que tiene que hacer es trabajar sobre el terreno y pelear por la presidencia de la diputación, la alcaldía de su ciudad o un escaño autonómico, no hacer pasillos en el Congreso' ('What a provincial party leader has to do is to get to work on the ground and fight to win control of the provincial executive or his town hall, or a seat in the AC assembly, not traipse around parliament').[8]

In keeping with its support for regional autonomy, the PP developed a federal structure, with branches at regional level and below, all endowed with similar institutions to the party at national level, but with the latter retaining overall control.[9] Aznar stressed the importance of adapting the party's internal structure and operation to what he called 'la realidad plural del estado autonómico' ('the plural reality of the autonomous state').[10] This allowed the party to become much stronger and more active in key parts of the country traditionally hostile to the old Francoist right.

Party ideology

The PP has always called itself 'liberal'. Castro refers to the pragmatic liberalism of the *Clan de Valladolid*, a group of economists who advised Aznar after he became president of the regional government of Castile-Leon in 1987.[11] Here he developed an anti-interventionist strategy and trimmed his administration, believing in the merits of 'un Estado pequeño y ágil en lugar de uno gordo e ineficiente' ('a small, trim state, not a fat, inefficient one').[12] Ross states that, if anything, the PP shifted away from Christian democrat ideas towards more liberal ones in terms of economic policy, which enabled it to regain the support of Spain's business confederation. He goes on to say that the resultant mix of social conservatism and economic liberalism brought it ideologically close to the British Tories, but in their contemporary, Thatcherite guise rather than the traditional brand which Fraga had always admired.[13] The PP therefore abandoned the Francoist policy of economic interventionism and placed privatization high on its agenda. Once in government, it sold off those state-owned companies with the most problems (Repsol, Endesa, Telefónica and Argentaria) and drew up a modernization programme for others such as Iberia, Hunosa and Santa Bárbara. Thatcherite influence was also apparent in the PP's 1993 manifesto, in which it promised to cut taxes while maintaining welfare spending and reducing the budgetary deficit. Brooksbank and O'Shaughnessy note that the PP often used the terms 'management', 'efficiency' and 'effectiveness' but always in connection with the private sector which it regarded as a model of efficiency.[14] According to *El País*, terms like 'efficiency', 'competitiveness', 'free market' and 'business criteria' frequently appear in the PP's policy documents.[15]

After Spain met the strict convergence criteria for EMU, the PP's economic policy did not change, especially as inflation fell to 2.2 per cent by 1998 (the lowest rate for twenty-nine years) and unemployment stood at 11 per cent (the lowest figure since 1982). Aznar stated that 'en dos años, la economía, la sociedad española, ha sido capaz de crear más de 800,000 nuevos puestos de trabajo estable y hemos superado el techo de 1974 de personas empleadas. Nosotros hemos cumplido los deberes: estamos en el euro, tenemos un déficit absolutamente controlado y nuestra economía crece a un ritmo muy fuerte' ('In two years Spanish society and the Spanish economy have managed to create over 800,000 permanent new jobs and we've beaten the 1974 record for the number of people employed. We've done our duty; we're in the euro, we've got our deficits under control and the economy is growing strongly').[16] It was largely on the strength of this economic performance that Aznar won the 2000 election with an overall majority.

The PP, although liberal on economic issues, is conservative when it comes to public morality. In the 1980s, the AP demanded the retention of capital punishment (especially for terrorist crime) and opposed divorce and the decriminalization of abortion, appealing unsuccessfully to the Constitutional Court on this issue. By contrast, the PP promised to annul no law passed since 1978, although it voted against the proposal to extend abortion for the mother with personal, social or family problems (the so-called fourth precondition or stipulation). To quote Mariano Rajoy: 'A nadie se le ocurre ahora manifestarse contra la ley del divorcio, se acepta la ley del aborto y no se considera a la homosexualidad como si fuera una cosa estratosférica' ('Nobody demonstrates against the abortion law now, the law on abortion was accepted and homosexuality is not seen as outlandish').[17] The PP toned down its manifesto demands for Basque terrorists to serve the full term of their prison sentences, when it was forced to enlist PNV support for its government programme after the 1996 general election. However, since winning an overall majority in 2000, it toughened its policy against Basque terrorism by introducing amendments to the law on political parties, which led to the banning of the political mouthpiece of *Euskadi Ta Askatasuna* (ETA), *Batasuna*, in August 2002, plunging relations with mainstream Basque parties to an all-time low.

The PP's greatest change has been in regional policy. In the early 1980s, Fraga argued repeatedly for reform of the autonomy section of the 1978 constitution and promised that an AP government would do away with the term *nacionalidades* and restrict the amount of autonomy for each region. However, after becoming leader of the regional government in Galicia, he advocated extending the powers of the ACs to bring the Spanish state closer to the vaguely federalist model inspired by the

The Partido Popular

West German system, and also suggested a single administrative structure whereby each region would control all levels of government bureaucracy within it.[18] The PP's commitment to maintain the autonomy system as laid down by the constitution has been strengthened by the fact that Aznar himself, like Mancha before him, was a product of that system, and Aznar has tenaciously defended the present system against the demands of his nationalist opponents, especially in the Basque Country. Rajoy too gained experience at regional level in Galicia, so party policy in this area is not likely to change under his leadership.

The moderate image which the PP seeks to project is associated with the centrist shift which has always been at the heart of its political philosophy. In fact, when Aznar became a member of the Spanish parliament in 1982, he promised to devote all his political and intellectual energies to reforming Spain's political centre.[19] The PP's slogan at its 10th congress in 1990 read *Centrados por la libertad* (Centrists through freedom), while three years later Alvarez Cascos opened the proceedings at its 11th congress by repeating the centrist views which Fraga had formulated way back in 1972: 'Si queremos evitar un posible bandazo a la izquierda, debemos marchar hacia el centro, por el camino de las reformas' ('If we want to avoid a lurch to the left, we must move towards the centre, by way of reforms'). In 1996, Aznar described his first cabinet as 'centrist and reformist' and, in anticipation of the PP's 13th congress and the new millennium, announced that '. . . el centro es el futuro. Es la reforma, la modernización, preparar el país para el siglo XXI' ('. . . the centre is the future. Reform and modernization will prepare the country for the twenty-first century').[20] At its 14th congress in January 2002, the PP was again defined as 'una formación política de centro reformista al servicio de los intereses generales de España' ('a centrist and reformist political structure focused on serving the general interests of Spain').

Much of the PP's centrism stems from the influence of former members of the UCD on the party. Charles Powell notes that almost half of the UCD's original executive was active in the PP in the 1990s.[21] Indeed, Calvo Sotelo and many former UCD ministers attended the PP's 12th congress in 1996. PP supporters remembered them as members of a clean and honest government pushed out of office by socialist sectarianism and rampant corruption and looked forward to Aznar rectifying this historical injustice. Former UCD members have been involved in the *Fundación para el Análisis y los Estudios Sociales*

(FAES), which was set up in May 1992 as the PP's equivalent of the Adam Smith Institute. Also top party figures such as Javier Arenas, Jaime Mayor Oreja and Soledad Becerril occupied important positions in the UCD hierarchy (the former two in Andalusia and the Basque Country respectively, and the latter as Spain's first female minister of culture).

The party also made a deliberate effort to woo the trade unions. Aznar's first meeting with the *Unión General de Trabajadores* (UGT) and *Comisiones Obreras* (CCOO) took place in December 1989, both unions sent representatives to the closing events at the PP's 11th and 13th congresses, and CCOO leader Antonio Gutiérrez and Aznar attended each other's congress in January 1996. The UGT leader Apolinar Rodríguez commented that the unions now had little to fear from the right because it no longer turned its back on them. However, the nationwide demonstrations organized in December 1998 in protest at the PP's social and fiscal policies (in particular, threats to unemployment protection and income tax reform) showed that the unions were still prepared to take defiant action against a right-wing government.[22] Labour relations from that point continued to deteriorate, with a general strike being declared in June 2002 against the government's reform of the unemployment benefit system.

The PP's opponents, however, still regard it as a right-wing party. In the 1993 general election, the PSOE played the *voto de miedo* card (the 'vote of fear'), warning voters that a PP victory would take the country back to Francoism. Then, during the 1996 campaign, it released a controversial video linking the PP to Opus Dei and the totalitarian right and hinting that Aznar had the full support of the Francoist hardliner Blas Piñar.[23] Indeed the presence of several PP government ministers at the ceremony to canonize the founder of Opus Dei in Rome in October 2002 suggested that there was still a connection between the PP and the extremely conservative Catholic lay order.

Party membership and age profile

In the 1990s, there were much younger faces in the PP hierarchy and among the delegates/representatives at its congresses. Federico Losantos refers to the emergence of 'un ejército de sombras, una generación fantasma de la que no sabemos prácticamente nada' which ousted the old right wing in a take-over without precedent in Europe ('an army of the shadows, a phantom generation, of which we know next to nothing').[24] He cites the case of Barrero Valverde as a typical example: having been a professional basketball player and member of the music group 'Los Trepidantes', he became a regional *diputado* in the PSOE stronghold of Extremadura before being elected to the presidency of the Senate in March 1996. In the aftermath of the 2000 general election, as William Chislett observes, few people personified better than the minister of education, Pilar del Castillo, the sociological sea change that allowed the PP to win an absolute majority. As a university rebel in the last years of the Franco dictatorship, she had formed part of a far-left clandestine cell.[25]

The rejuvenation of the party went hand in hand with an increase in membership, from 186,000 in 1989 to 584,000 in 1999, making it Spain's largest party by far. In 1995, it had 900 offices, 400 more than in 1990. In 1996, it claimed to be consolidating its influence in every province and social sector, recording a particularly healthy growth in the Basque Country, where its members formed the youngest branch of the party. The greatest concentration of members has always been in Madrid and other large cities such as Valencia, Alicante and Murcia – proof of the PP's ability to penetrate urban areas, where the PSOE was traditionally strong. Students form 15 per cent of the membership, and women 25 per cent, while few members are under twenty-three or over fifty-five.[26]

Election performance

Since its relaunch, the PP displayed a rising electoral profile. In the 1989 general election, Aznar succeeded in breaking through Fraga's '*techo electoral*' (electoral ceiling) and won more votes than Felipe González in Madrid. In the municipal elections of May 1991, the PP took control of Madrid, Seville, Valencia and sixteen provincial capitals, making inroads into traditional socialist heartlands. CDS's heavy losses led to the resignation of Adolfo Suárez the following October, enabling Aznar to claim all the ground to the right of Felipe González for himself. In 1993, the 141 seats won by the PP confirmed Aznar as a serious challenger to González, especially after he had won one of the *teleduelos* (television debates) that were held prior to the election.

With the PSOE mired in corruption and the GAL (*Grupos Antiterroristas de Liberación* – Antiterrorist Liberation Groups) controversy[27], the real breakthough for the PP came with the 1994 European election. Achieving a 40 per cent share of the vote, it at last beat the PSOE in a national election. Also, in the Andalusian election, it gained fifteen seats and the PSOE lost its majority. Significantly, Javier Arenas, who was the party's regional leader at the time, did not mention the word *derecha* (right-wing) once during his campaign, but expressed admiration for the UCD and Christian democracy. Later that year in the Basque election PP won eleven seats (four in Alava, three in Guipúzcoa and four in Vizcaya), five more than in 1990, and it obtained the most votes in San Sebastián. In the regional and municipal elections of May 1995, it maintained its momentum, winning an absolute majority in thirty-three provincial capitals and emerging as the leading party in another ten, as well as in twelve of the thirteen autonomous regions and 3,500 of the 8,000 municipalities. It took control even of the leftist strongholds of Córdoba and Asturias, taking advantage of the disunity between the PSOE and *Izquierda Unida* (IU – United Left). These elections were also a triumph for the PP's female politicians like Celia Villalobos, Teófila Martínez and Luisa Rudí, all of whom had gained experience in the *Cortes* before ousting the PSOE from its traditional power bases in Málaga, Cádiz and Zaragoza respectively.[28] Then, in November 1995, the PP achieved its best ever result in Catalonia, gaining ten seats and preventing *Convergència i Unió* (CiU) from retaining its overall majority. In 1999, it found itself in the unaccustomed position of keeping the CiU in the *Generalitat* by virtue of coming third together with *Esquerra Republicana de Catalunya* (ERC) in the regional elections that year and preventing the Catalan socialists from taking power.

One worrying sign for the PP has been its consistently high level of voter rejection, even more than that of *Herri Batasuna* on the Basque extreme left. For instance, in 1995, at least half of those polled did not want the PP to win the next general election, even though the PSOE was mired in scandal. In addition, the rural and elderly vote was stubbornly behind the socialists, especially in Andalusia and Extremadura where unemployment benefits had been distributed under the Rural Employment Plan, which the PP criticized as 'a politically motivated expenditure of state funds that enabled the PSOE to rely on a "captive vote"'.[29] These factors explain why the PP's margin of victory in the 1996 general election was so narrow, with just over 1 per cent in the share of the vote separating it from the PSOE. In fact, it was only because of a split in the left-wing vote that the PP gained decisive seats in nine constituencies. In the Andalusian election on the same day, the PP lost one seat, because of the strength of the PSOE support in rural areas.

Since gaining power nationally, the PP consolidated its position in Galicia, with Fraga being re-elected in 1997 and again in 2001 with an overall majority. In spite of his increasing infirmity (he was eighty years old in 2002), he decided to stand yet again in 2005. However, the fallout from the regional and national governments' mishandling of the *Prestige* oil disaster of November 2002 were among the factors that led to a change of government with a coalition of socialists and the nationalist BNG taking control of the region in the June 2005 elections. Meanwhile, in the Basque Country, the PP continued its electoral advance, coming second behind the *Partido Nacionalista Vasco* (PNV – the Basque Nationalist Party) in the 2000 general election and winning outright in San Sebastián and Vitoria. Its 250,580 votes were the highest ever recorded for a right-wing party in that troubled part of the country. Consequently, it had high hopes of victory when the Basque president, Juan José Ibarretxe, was forced to call an early election in May 2001. However, despite the presence of Jaime Mayor Oreja as the PP candidate and a leading advocate of a hard line against Basque terrorist violence, the PNV were returned to power with a 43 per cent share of the vote because many Basques feared the consequences of an unprecedented PP victory.

In the 1999 municipal, regional and European elections, the PP managed to consolidate rather than improve on the successes it had achieved in 1995. Faced with a resurgent PSOE that was able to attract many IU voters, it lost one MEP and its share of the vote dropped by less than 1 per cent. It held on to most of its regional governments, with the notable exceptions of Asturias, where the PSOE regained control, and the Balearic Islands, where it surrendered power to a new left-wing, nationalist and ecological coalition. At municipal level, it lost ground in its traditional strongholds of La Coruña, Lugo, Cuenca, Guadalajara, Segovia, Soria and Granada.

The PP's greatest triumph to date came with its absolute majority in the 2000 general election. Its 183 seats in the Congress, ten million votes and first place in forty-two of Spain's fifty-two constituencies secured victory on a par with that of the PSOE in 1982. Charles Powell observes that 'el PP estaba ya razonablemente implantado en todo el territorio, convirtiéndose finalmente en lo que había representado el PSOE en 1982: un partido verdaderamente nacional' ('the PP was already reasonably well implanted across the whole of Spain, repeating the feat achieved by the PSOE in 1982 in becoming a truly national party').[30] In the municipal and regional elections of May 2003, the PP performed above expectations, holding its ground despite public anger at Aznar's support for the US-led war on Iraq and running the PSOE close in the overall share of the vote. Alberto Ruiz-Gallardón won the coveted mayoral race in Madrid with the help of Aznar's wife, Ana Botella, who became a city councillor, although this success was counter-balanced by the loss of the regional government in the Comunidad de Madrid, which Ruiz-Gallardón had previously led, to an alliance between the PSOE and IU – a result which was subsequently reversed in PP's favour when two PSOE representatives pulled out.

Autonomy policy

Under Aznar's premiership changes were made to the so-called 'slow track' autonomy statutes, enabling all the ACs to achieve equality in basic public services by the end of 1998. According to Mariano Rajoy, these reforms provided a stable basis on which each community could legally exercise the full extent of its powers under the constitution.[31] This is why the PP reacted strongly against the *Declaración de Barcelona*, which was drawn up in July 1998 by the main nationalist parties in Catalonia, the Basque Country and Galicia to press for self-determination for the three historic nationalities. It condemned their agreement as 'una acción conjunta para configurar un Estado plurinacional de tipo confederal' ('a combined operation aiming to turn Spain into a multinational state on confederal lines'), and Rajoy reminded them that their existing powers under the constitution were greater than those of the *Länder* of Germany, the most decentralized country in Europe.[32] The leaders of the PP's regional governments, along with Carlos Iturgaiz, the Basque PP leader, later signed their own declaration in San Sebastián, stating that the constitution and autonomy statutes were the proper channels of self-government for the different ACs and genuinely reflected Spain's pluralism.[33]

On the matter of financial relationships between the centre and periphery, the PP's policy has not been as clear or consistent. At its 11th congress, it approved the transfer of 15 per cent of income tax to the regions, but when this was implemented by the PSOE government, the PP's leaders condemned it as a concession to the Catalan *Generalitat*. Fraga even appealed to the Constitutional Court on behalf of Galicia which, as an economically weaker region, would be disadvantaged by this new arrangement. However, after May 1995, when the PP gained control of most of the regional governments, it tacitly accepted the new system, as it was clear that areas like Madrid, La Rioja and Valencia could benefit. Rajoy explained the PP's position thus: 'El apoyo no equivale a conformidad, sino un gesto de responsabilidad para facilitar la gobernabilidad' ('Support doesn't mean agreement; rather it's showing responsibility, making it easier to govern').[34] Finally, in the protracted negotiations with the Catalans after the 1996 election, Aznar raised the proportion of income tax revenue to 30 per cent in order to secure CiU support for his government. He also agreed that the regions could share central government's tax-raising powers – even though none of this had appeared in the PP's manifesto – and gave the Basques the same degree of fiscal autonomy that applied to Navarre, including taxation on alcohol, tobacco and fuel. Fraga, for his part, did a U-turn, coming out in support of the 30 per cent figure and withdrawing his appeal to the Constitutional Court. His argument was that the latest changes satisfied his demands for 'suficiencia, solidaridad, igualdad en los servicios esenciales mínimos, autonomía financiera y corresponsabilidad' ('sufficiency, solidarity, equality in provision of minimum essential services, financial autonomy and responsibility on both sides').[35]

Regional activities

After years of marginalization in the Basque Country, the PP's fortunes were transformed in the 1994 regional election, when, under the leadership of Jaime Mayor Oreja, it doubled its parliamentary representation (from six to eleven seats) and established a rudimentary party organization in the rural areas of Vizcaya and Guipúzcoa. However, ETA reacted by targeting local PP officials. In January 1995 it assassinated Gregorio Ordóñez, PP leader in Guipúzcoa and deputy mayor of San Sebastián, and in July 1997 kidnapped and murdered

Miguel Angel Blanco, the young Ermua councillor. As a result, the PP was driven virtually underground in the region, fearful for the survival of its activists. Strangely, party recruitment increased after the assassination of Ordóñez, and the membership of *Nuevas Generaciones*, the youth section to which Blanco belonged, went up from 955 to 1,230 after his kidnap. As William Chislett observes, the PP's unequivocal stance against ETA won it supporters from a population tired of more than thirty years of political violence.[36] However, this support was not strong enough to enable the PP, with the help of the socialists, to wrest power from the PNV in 2001 – a result which showed how polarized and fractured Basque society had become.

Problems of a different kind affected the PP in Catalonia. In its AP days, it underwent frequent changes of regional leader and its election results were consistently poor, losing the non-nationalist vote to the PSOE and centre-right support to the CiU. However, Aleix Vidal-Quadras led the PP to a respectable third place in the 1995 regional election on a radical, anti-nationalist ticket and attracted support from voters who were not happy with the González–Pujol pact. However, as a result of Aznar's deal with Pujol following the 1996 general election, Vidal-Quadras was forced to quit the Catalan leadership at Aznar's insistence, but not before he had publicly denounced the PP's pact with the CiU as bare-faced opportunism.[37] At its 9th congress in September 2000, the Catalan PP accepted the programme of *catalanismo integrador* put forward by Josep Piqué, its new political heavyweight and the then minister of foreign affairs. It renamed itself the *Partit Popular de Catalunya* (PPC), so as to confirm its conversion to moderate catalanism – a catalanist movement that regarded Catalonia as an integral part of Spain's national identity.[38]

Up to 1995, Cantabria suffered all that was wrong with the Spanish centre-right. It was plagued by UCD factionalism, its first president resigned because of pressures in Fraga's *Coalición Popular*, and Juan Hormaechea, an AP independent who took over the government in June 1987, publicly insulted the national leadership and created his own breakaway party, *Unión para el Progreso de Cantabria* (UPCA). Little wonder, then, that the Cantabrians held their politicians in low regard. On at least six occasions PP spurned the opportunity to get rid of Hormaechea but feared losing the region to the socialists. Eventually, Hormaechea was banned from political activity for four years in 1995, after insulting a local mayor, and the PP at last beat the UPCA in the May election of that year to regain the government. In

2003, they were unseated by an alliance between the PSOE and the *Partido Regionalista de Cantabria* (PRC), whose leader Miguel Angel Revilla became president, even though his party had only come third in the election and supported the PP regional government for the previous eight years.

Like Cantabria, the Balearic Islands were from the outset a right-wing stronghold, but, until 1995, its government remained free from the kind of crisis that had afflicted the PP in Santander. It was an extremely prosperous region, with the local economy dominated by a vibrant tourist industry, and with private enterprise and regional government collaborating successfully. Gabriel Cañellas, who came to power in 1983, governed initially in coalition with *Unió Mallorquina* (UM), but gradually built up a solid and loyal party network which allowed him to remain in power until 1995, by which time his administration had become a model for others to follow. However, following a police investigation into the payment of fifty million pesetas into the bank accounts of local PP leaders by the company constructing the Sóller tunnel on Majorca, Cañellas was forced to resign. His successor, Cristòfol Soler, had a torrid year in office. Having tried to implement linguistic, environmental and union-friendly policies, he fell out with the PP group in parliament, led by Cañellas, and was replaced by Jaume Matas. After the 1999 regional elections the PP lost out to a coalition led by the PSOE, which included the Greens and the UM. However, Matas, having served a term in national government as environment minister, regained control for the PP in May 2003 in a coalition with the UM, but came under immediate pressure to repeal the controversial tourist tax introduced by the previous administration.

Galicia, another region controlled by the AP in the 1980s, suffered the ultimate embarrassment of its president Fernández Albor being voted out of office in 1987 following the resignation of his deputy Xosé Luis Barreiro and other members of the AP government who then formed a coalition with the socialists. However, Fraga restored his party to power in 1989 with an overall majority and calmed the troubled waters, transforming the region into an independent and seemingly impregnable PP power base. From then on, he remained a veritable paterfamilias, keeping the traditional territorial rivalries of the Galician right in check, and became a confirmed *galeguista*, proud of the investment made in the region's basic infrastructure and seizing every opportunity to promote Galicia on the international stage. For years there has been speculation about who will succeed him and whether territorial rivalries and power struggles will re-emerge. For a time, the favourite was the regional general secretary, Xosé Cuiña, who succeeded in curbing the influence of the two Madrid-based leaders, Romay Beccaría and Rajoy, on the executive committee at the regional congress in June 1998. However, he was made the scapegoat for the PP's poor electoral performance in the 1999 municipal elections, in which its nationalist rival the BNG took control of the councils of Vigo, Pontevedra and El Ferrol. This enabled Rajoy, who became a key figure in the Aznar government after the 2000 general election, to re-establish his influence in the region. Under his authority and with Fraga's approval, changes of leadership were made at provincial and municipal level and Xesús Palmou was appointed as the new regional secretary with the task of achieving consensus between Madrid headquarters and the local party barons. [39] Palmou managed Fraga's successful election campaign in 2001 and stands in for him on the PP's national executive, so he must be considered Fraga's most likely successor.

In Asturias and Murcia, two of the PP's conquests in 1995, its experiences could not be more contrasting. In Murcia, Ramón Valcárcel took over from the old AP leader, Juan Ramón Calero, renewed the party from top to bottom and defeated the socialists by the largest majority in the 1995 elections. With a cost-cutting budget to ease the region's debt and strong support for the highly controversial National Hydrological Plan to divert water from the River Ebro, Valcárcel's government has gone from strength to strength, being returned to power in 2003 with a thumping majority. Meanwhile, in Asturias, a region with strong socialist connections, Sergio Marqués gained power unexpectedly for the PP in 1995, thanks to left-wing disunity. However, relationships between his government and the regional party deteriorated so badly that in 1998 he and six of his councillors were suspended from the PP membership and lost the confidence of their parliamentary group. Matters were made worse when eighteen of the PP's twenty-two mayors in the region protested at the way in which Alvarez Cascos, their national MP and the then party secretary, had been interfering in their affairs and sided with Marqués. The conflict began as a squabble over who should take the credit for investment in the region, but it then mushroomed into a bitter power struggle between Marqués on the one hand and Cascos and local party leader Fernández Rozada on the other. In February 1999, Marqués, four

suspended councillors and seven ex-PP mayors launched their own
new party, *Unión Renovadora Asturiana* (URAS), calling it 'un
partido centrado, liberal, moderno y regionalista' ('a modern liberal,
regionalist party of the centre').[40] As a Marqués supporter remarked,
'nunca será un partido centralista y sometido a los dictados de un
despacho de Madrid, como hasta ahora ha sido el PP de Asturias' ('it
will never be a centralist party at the beck and call of Madrid, as the
PP in Asturias has been up till now).[41] In the subsequent regional
election on 13 June, three URAS members won seats and the PSOE
regained power with an overall majority. In 2003, the PP, led by
former senator Ovidio Sánchez, staged an impressive recovery, profiting
from the decline of the URAS to come close to ousting the socialists.

Figure 1.1: The Partido Popular in the Basque Country, Electoral Performance
1980–2001

Election	Mar 1980	Feb 1984	Nov 1986	Oct 1990	Oct 1994	Oct 1998	May 2001
Nº Seats	2*	7**	4**	6	11	16	19***
Vote %	5	10	8	9	14	20	23

*as AP   **as AP/CP   ***in coalition with UA (Unidad Alavesa)

Figure 1.2: The Partido Popular in Catalonia, Electoral Performance 1980–2003

Election	Mar 1980	April 1984	May 1988	Mar 1992	Nov 1995	Oct 1999	Nov 2003
Nº Seats	0*	11**	6***	7	17	12	15
Vote %	2	8	5	6	13	9	12

*as Solidaridad Catalana   **as AP/CP   ***as AP

Figure 1.3: The Partido Popular in Galicia, Electoral Performance 1980–2001

Election	Oct 1981	Nov 1985	Dec 1989	Oct 1993	Oct 1997	Oct 2001
Nº Seats	26*	35**	38	42	42	41
Vote %	30	41	45	52	52	51

*as AP   **as AP/CP

Relations with other parties

Over the years the PP has formed pacts with smaller regionalist parties in order to avoid the problems of minority administrations, and actually merged its organization with the *Unión del Pueblo Navarro* (UPN) in Navarre in March 1991. It formed pacts with the *Partido Aragonés Regionalista* (PAR) in Aragon, *Unión Valenciana* (UV) in Valencia and *Partido Regionalista Cántabro* (PRC) in Cantabria. However, in 1999 the PAR accused the PP of not representing Aragon's interests properly in Madrid and formed a coalition with the socialists instead, while in 2003 the PRC and the PSOE collaborated to prevent the PP from returning to power in Cantabria (see previous section).

Having fought the Basque and Catalan parties in every election since 1977 and castigated Felipe González for his agreement with Jordi Pujol in 1993, the PP found itself having to rely on the Basques and Catalans for parliamentary support after the 1996 elections. Interior minister Jaime Mayor Oreja believed that good relations between the government and the PNV were crucial for peace in the Basque Country and for the fight against ETA terrorism. However, the PNV's subsequent involvement in the *Declaración de Barcelona* and the *Pacto de Estella* with the HB put paid to any further collaboration with the PP. Carlos Iturgaiz, the regional PP leader, declared that the PNV had become part of the Basque liberation movement, while the PNV savaged the PP for its links with the Franco regime.[42] The ending of the ETA ceasefire in December 1999 set the parties even further apart, with the PP accusing the PNV of being an apologist for separatist violence and PNV pursuing a pro-sovereignty line more actively.[43] Since then there has been even greater polarization. In September 2000, the PP and the PSOE unsuccessfully tabled a censure motion against the PNV government and signed an anti-terrorist pact the following December, demanding that the PNV sever all ties with the separatist left. Relations hit an all-time low in 2002 when the PNV fiercely opposed the government ban on *Batasuna* and voted against the amendments to the law on political parties which allowed the government to ban any group which 'promoted hatred, violence and civil conflict'. The PNV's subsequent proposal to redefine the autonomous status of the Basque Country and hold a referendum on this issue was immediately challenged by the PP as contrary to the constitution.

Aznar's pact with Jordi Pujol in 1996 was a bitter pill for many PP activists to swallow. Until then, they had criticized Pujol for having propped up the PSOE government, vehemently opposed the CiU government in the *Generalitat* and personally insulted Pujol on election night in March 1996 with the offensive chant of 'Pujol, enano, aprenda castellano' ('Pujol, you dwarf, learn Castilian'). Aznar found himself having to tone down this aggressive anti-nationalism in his party by persuading Aleix Vidal-Quadras, the PP's strident leader in Catalonia, to resign and make way for the more emollient Alberto Fernández Díaz. The rapprochement between Aznar and Pujol was made possible through the mediation of Antoni Duran i Lleida, the *Unió Democràtica de Catalunya* (UDC) leader and Pujol's Christian democrat partner who had originally persuaded Pujol to break his pact with the PSOE and bring forward the 1996 election. The CiU maintained its support for the PP's economic policy for the full term of the first PP government, especially as it was forced to rely on the PP to keep its own minority government in power after 1999 in the *Generalitat*. However, Pujol's long-term ambitions to obtain full tax-raising powers for Catalonia and raise its status to that of a nation state gave rise to heated opposition in the PP and reignited the traditional animosity between Barcelona and Madrid. In the summer of 2000, for example, official cars belonging to the *Generalitat* carried the 'CAT' initials on the new European number plates in defiance of orders from the central PP government. The more radical stance of Artur Mas, Pujol's successor as leader of the CiU, is likely to make future relations difficult between the two parties at both regional and national level, although the present pact between the socialists and the ERC in Catalonia could bring both centre-right parties closer together again.

PP and Europe

Ever since its change of name to the designation adopted by Christian democratic parties in other European countries, there can be no doubting PP's commitment to the European Union, and there is little sign of the kind of euroscepticism rampant among British Conservatives. Aznar always regarded his contribution to Spain's involvement in European integration as one of his basic responsibilities.[44] His first move was to increase the PP's participation in the European People's Party (EPP), which he saw as one of the most important organizations in the EU and a strong supporter for the PP's position outside Spain.[45] He also continued PP's membership of the International Democratic Union, which the AP joined in 1983. However, the PP's affiliation to the EPP encountered opposition from the PNV and the Christian democrats in the CiU which condemned its Francoist origins, while the old AP guard led by Fernando Suárez and Robles Piquer saw the move as a dilution of the party's conservatism. The EPP leader Wilfried Martens was consistently supportive of Aznar, and prior to the 1996 election made a point of declaring total confidence in Aznar's European policies and his suitability as a future EU president. Aznar also built up a close relationship with Helmut Kohl and the CDU, while Jacques Chirac was the first foreign leader to back Aznar in the 1993 elections by wishing him the same success for the centre-right in Spain as it had achieved in France the previous March. The British Tories were disappointed at Aznar's failure to win power in 1993, as John Major hoped Aznar would be a potential right-wing ally against the European federalism that Felipe González had been promoting.

However, as regards Spain and Europe, there is little to differentiate the PP from the PSOE. Brooksbank and O'Shaughnessy note that both parties equate 'Europe' with 'modernity' and have espoused a largely uncritical commitment to the EU, the single market and economic and monetary union, while pledging to defend Spanish interests, especially in agriculture.[46]

After coming to power in 1996, Aznar continued from where Felipe González left off, pulling out all the stops to achieve European integration. Indeed, he believed it was his mission to put Spain onto the European 'fast track' and put an end to Spaniards being regarded as second-class Europeans. By applying a tight budgetary policy, he succeeded in achieving Spain's EMU membership in the first round. His 1997 Stability Plan (*Programa de Convergencia* 1997–2000) went for strong economic growth (3.2 per cent average per year), high levels of private investment, increased privatization and large-scale job creation. In the 1998 'state of the nation' debate, with Spain having met all the convergence criteria within the space of two years, a triumphalist Aznar 'envuelto en la bandera del euro' ('wrapped in the flag of the euro') declared that Spaniards were now reaping the benefits of his policies.[47] However, try as he might to change Spain into one of the most modern and attractive countries in Europe, the fact remains that it is not a net payer like Germany and is still numbered among the poorer nations, albeit the biggest and toughest of these.

As far as his ideas on EU development were concerned, Aznar strongly favoured decentralization and subsidiarity (his adoption of Fraga's single administrative structure reflected this) and was keen for all EU institutions to follow his drive for austerity.[48] In August 1996, his government took steps to achieve greater participation of the Autonomous Communities in European affairs by creating the post of autonomic attaché in Brussels. Also, Aznar saw Spain as the principal promoter of Latin American interests in the EU, and in October 1998 proposed the creation of a special fund for Latin America to which Spain would contribute.

In Strasbourg, the AP's representatives had previously sat with the British Conservatives, but after the change of party name Fraga agreed that they would join the Christian democrat EPP group, which was by far the largest on the centre-right.[49] In October 1991 the PP became a full member of the EPP, despite opposition from the old conservatives in the party and the traditional Christian Democrats in the PNV and the UDC. Aznar's election as an EPP vice-president in 1993 gave him the ideal opportunity to raise his international profile, and the EPP leaders strongly endorsed his 1993 election campaign by holding a special meeting in Valencia just before the elections. That same year, the PP also joined the Christian Democrat International (CDI) and linked up with centre parties in Latin American countries. With the defeat of Helmut Kohl as German Chancellor, Aznar became the sole right-wing survivor among EU leaders and advocated opening up the EPP to liberal and conservative influences. For example, it was at Aznar's instigation that Silvio Berlusconi's *Forza Italia* (FI) party joined the group, much to the displeasure of the Christian democrats who believed that the FI's populist and liberal ideology was incompatible with the EPP's basic principles of social justice and Christian humanism. In November 2001 Aznar was unanimously elected to the presidency of the CDI, thus completing his rise as an international statesman. The person responsible for paving the way for Aznar's nomination was Alejandro Agag, one of the PP's young MEPs who had been elected general secretary of the CDI in October 2000. When he stepped down in 2002 to take up a post in a Portuguese bank and marry Aznar's daughter, he was replaced by another young PP politician, Antonio López-Istúriz, confirming the strong influence of the PP in higher reaches of the EPP and the CDI.

Conclusions

Although the PP government had for various reasons become unpopular in Aznar's second term, the opinion polls before the 2004 general election indicated that it would be re-elected, mainly because of the high growth rate and the steady increase in living standards that had been achieved since 2000. However, the horrendous terrorist attack in Madrid three days before the elections were held, transformed the political situation, and as a result of popular anger at the PP government's blatant attempt to pin the blame for the atrocity on ETA, the PSOE was catapulted back into power at the PP's expense. Despite the shock of defeat, there were few if any recriminations within the party, and Mariano Rajoy maintained his position as party leader. Indeed the morale of the party was quite high, judging from the upbeat tone at its 15th national congress which was held in Madrid the following October under the banner '*España, la ilusión que nos une*' ('Spain, the hope that unites us').

It remains to be seen how effective the PP will be in opposition over the next three years but at least it has its strength and organization to draw on, even in the 'problem areas' of the Basque Country and Catalonia. Furthermore, it has made itself attractive to many of Spain's younger voters. As Juan Manuel Moreno, president of *Nuevas Generaciones*, remarked after the 2000 election, for the first time since the democratic transition a party in government did not lose the support of young voters, but saw it rise to over 65 per cent of this section of the electorate.[50] On an international level too the PP became a powerful force under Aznar's leadership. It exported its centrist ideology to organizations such as the EPP and CDI, modified their traditional Christian democrat ethos and broadened the international centre-right movement. Although Aznar attracted criticism for having aligned himself closely with Blair and Bush in the Iraqi war, it cannot be denied that he put himself and his party on the world stage – a notable first for a Spanish right-wing leader. All these factors suggest that the PP is in a healthy position to mount an effective challenge to the PSOE next time round and will remain a potent force in Spanish politics for years to come.

Notes

[1] For a full account of the rise of the party, see my book, *Manuel Fraga Iribarne and the rebirth of Spanish* Conservatism *1939–1990* (Lewiston: Mellen, 1999).

[2] Julia Navarro, *Entre Felipe y Aznar. 1982–1996* (Madrid: Temas de Hoy, 1996), p. 169.

[3] Luis Herrero, *El Poder Popular* (Madrid: Temas de Hoy, 1996), p. 48.

[4] Graciano Palomo, *El vuelo del halcón* (Madrid: Temas de Hoy, 1990), p. 422.

[5] Herrero, p. 8.

[6] Raimundo Castro, *El sucesor* (Madrid: Espasa-Calpe, 1995), pp. 55–6.

[7] Mercedes de la Merced was subsequently replaced by Eugenio Nasarre.

[8] El País, 14 August 1993.

[9] Michael T. Newton and Peter J. Donaghy, *Institutions of Modern Spain. A Political and Economic Guide* (Cambridge UP, 1997), pp. 202–3.

[10] José María Aznar, *España. La segunda transición* (Madrid: Espasa-Calpe, 1994), p. 86.

[11] Castro, p. 91.

[12] Herrero, p. 119.

[13] Christopher Ross, *Contemporary Spain. A Handbook* (London: Arnold, 1997), pp. 65–6.

[14] Anny Brooksbank and Martin O'Shaughnessy, 'Policy, rhetoric and the 1993 Spanish election campaign', *ACIS*, 6, 2 (1993), 10–11.

[15] El País, 27 November 1994.

[16] Ibid, 11 October 1998.

[17] Castro, p. 103.

[18] Gilmour, Manuel Fraga Iribarne p.318. In the first two years of PP government, some 131 million pesetas were saved, with central government moving out of some fifty-five of its regional offices.

[19] Aznar, p. 20.

[20] John Gilmour, '*La Odisea de Querer ser Centrista*: contrasting fortunes in the evolution of the democratic right in Spain since 1976', *IJIS*, 13, 1 (2000), 41.

[21] Charles Powell, *España en democracia, 1975–2000* (Barcelona: Plaza y Janés, 2001), p. 569 (1n).

[22] Ibid, 4 December 1998.

[23] Gilmour, *Odisea*, 43.

[24] Herrero, iii–iv.

[25] William Chislett, *Spain at a Glance 2001* (Madrid: Banco Santander Central Hispano, 2000), p. 55.

[26] ABC, 27 July 1998.

[27] These were secret military operations against Basque militants conducted by shadowy groups close to the police (Guardia Civil) apparently with the knowledge and connivance of the Socialist government.

[28] Rudí, together with former Education Minister Esperanza Aguirre, completed a notable double in 2000, when they became the first women to hold the presidencies of the two chambers of the *Cortes*.

[29] Jonathan Hopkin, 'An incomplete alternation: the Spanish elections of March 1996', *IJIS*, 9, 2 (1996), 115.

[30] Powell, p. 619.
[31] ABC, 7 September 1998.
[32] El País, 20 July 1998.
[33] ABC, 4 October 1998.
[34] El País, 4 October 1995.
[35] La Vanguardia, 3 May 1996.
[36] Chislett, p. 56.
[37] Vidal-Quadras remained as a member of PP's national executive. At the end of July 1999 he was replaced as the general co-ordinator of FAES after becoming a MEP.
[38] El Mundo, 16 September 2000.
[39] El País, 22 May 2000.
[40] Ibid, 21 February 1999.
[41] Ibid, 24 November 1998.
[42] El País, 30 September 1998. Also Gilmour, *Odisea*, 43.
[43] Chislett, p. 231.
[44] Aznar, p. 160.
[45] Navarro, p. 345.
[46] Brooksbank and O'Shaughnessy, 9.
[47] El País, 13 May 1998.
[48] Aznar, pp. 166–7.
[49] Ross, p. 66.
[50] El Mundo, 21 March 2000.

2

The Spanish Socialist Party (PSOE)

PAUL KENNEDY

1. General information about the PSOE

1.1 Historical Background: 1879–1975

The *Partido Socialista Obrero Español* (Spanish Socialist Workers Party – PSOE) was established in Madrid in 1879 by a group of printers. The early PSOE was notable for its derivative, simplistic understanding of Marxist theory and its adherence to a legalistic, reformist practice, albeit with frequent recourse to revolutionary rhetoric.[1] The trade union wing of the socialist movement, the *Unión General de Trabajadores* (General Workers' Union – UGT), was founded in 1888. Growth was largely restricted to the socialist heartlands of Madrid, Asturias and the Basque Country and the PSOE only gained its first parliamentary representative in 1910.

Despite a split caused by the departure of pro-Bolshevik members who left to found the *Partido Comunista de España* (Spanish Communist Party – PCE) in 1921, the PSOE had increased its number of parliamentary representatives to seven by 1923. When Primo de Rivera ended the corrupt Restoration system with his *coup d'état* the same year, the socialist leadership opted to collaborate with the dictatorship, thereby enabling the socialist movement to escape the repression visited upon its anarchist and communist rivals. When popular support for the regime waned in the context of the international economic crisis of the late 1920s, the socialists distanced themselves from the regime and placed themselves at the head of a broad anti-monarchist coalition which declared the Second Republic in April 1931.

By now the best-organized and most popular political party in Spain, the PSOE contributed three ministers to the government of the Republic which sought to implement an ambitious programme of social and political reforms. This agenda was nevertheless frustrated by the land-based reactionary elites, whose representatives won elections held towards the end of 1933 and set about reversing the progressive legislation enacted during the Republic's early years. The left returned to power in the form of the Popular Front in February 1936 and thereafter political tension grew throughout the country until the outbreak of civil war in July 1936.

Although the PSOE provided the Republic with two prime ministers during the Civil War, Francisco Largo Caballero and Juan Negrín, the party increasingly found itself eclipsed by the Communist Party in the prosecution of the war effort. Franco's victory over the Republic in 1939 left the PSOE broken, divided and facing an uncertain future.

In the wake of the Civil War, the party's structures proved to be poorly suited to the style of clandestine political activity mastered by the more effective Communist Party. Six entire executive committees were arrested and imprisoned by the Francoist authorities during the late 1940s and early 1950s and the prominent socialist leader, Tomás Centeno, was tortured and killed by the security forces in 1953.

Forced into exile in Toulouse, the party leadership became increasingly out of touch with developments within a Spain which, by the 1960s, was undergoing a profound socio-economic transformation. Nevertheless, a younger generation of activists from within Spain succeeded in wresting control from the exiled leadership and the 32 year old Felipe González was voted leader at the party's 26th congress in 1974, the last PSOE congress to be held in exile. The following year Franco died.

1.2 From Party in Exile to Party in Power: 1975–82

Receiving crucial financial support from other European social demo-cratic parties, particularly the West German Social Democratic Party (SPD), the PSOE rapidly established a nationwide party apparatus. Anxious not to be outflanked on the left by the larger and better organized Communist Party, the PSOE leadership fostered a radical image, in which the party's Marxist heritage was emphasized. Despite the party's surprisingly strong showing at the general election held in June 1977, when the PSOE became the second largest party in the Spanish Congress, a feat which it repeated at the March 1979 general election, the leadership concluded that the party's Marxist label was hindering further electoral progress. Felipe González consequently advised that the party drop its Marxist self-definition at the PSOE's 28th congress in May 1979. When members voted down his motion,

González stunned everyone by resigning the leadership in protest. Aware that González was the PSOE's prime electoral asset, the membership nevertheless ensured that he was re-elected as leader at an extraordinary congress later that year. The party thereafter ceased to describe itself primarily in Marxist terms and the PSOE established itself as a moderate centre-left party. The image of moderation and stability presented by the PSOE was particularly important in the context of the disintegration of the centre-right *Unión de Centro Democrático* (Democratic Centre Union – UCD) following its victory at the 1979 general election.[2] The failed *coup d'état* of February 1981 further underlined the PSOE's significance as an alternative party of government capable of safeguarding Spain's democratic future.

The scale of the PSOE's victory at the general election held in October 1982 – the party obtained just under half of the vote and 58 per cent of parliamentary seats – enabled it to form a single party government for the first time in its history. Furthermore, with its electoral support well distributed around the country, the party attracted voters from across the electoral spectrum, thereby confirming its evolution into a 'catch-all' party. Just one fifth of its votes came from the manual working class, whilst the party gained more votes than any other party in all professional and employed sectors of the population with the exception of owners of small- and medium-sized enterprises. Furthermore, the proportion of party members from professional and white-collar sectors of the community also grew significantly. Essentially, the party's socialism was now viewed in terms of accepting the challenge of consolidating Spanish democracy whilst at the same time bringing Spain up to the level of its European neighbours.

1.3 The PSOE in Office: 1982–96

The most urgent task facing the incoming PSOE government was the tackling of the decade-long economic crisis which had only been partially addressed by the previous UCD government. Unlike their French counterparts, the Spanish socialists rejected the implementation of an expansionary economic policy in favour of a tough, fiscally orthodox approach aimed at securing the country's membership of the European Community before the end of the party's first four-year term in office. The PSOE viewed European integration as providing the framework for securing the country's 'modernization', a constant theme throughout the party's entire period in office.

Membership of the European Community was duly secured in January 1986, albeit at the cost of a deterioration in relations with the trade unions as the government's industrial policies led to mass redundancies. The PSOE leadership's volte-face on Spain's membership of NATO also paid off when Spaniards narrowly voted to remain in the alliance in a referendum held in March 1986. The momentum provided by the referendum result contributed towards the PSOE winning the general election held three months later.

Entry into the European Community coincided with, and aided, a five-year period of economic growth in Spain, which outstripped that enjoyed by all other EC countries. Despite the scale of the economic boom, the government refused to devote significantly more resources to social welfare. In response, the trade unions, including the socialist UGT, called a one-day general strike in December 1988, which obtained massive support from the Spanish population. As Joaquín Almunia, PSOE general secretary between 1997 and 2000 has admitted, the shock occasioned by the general strike led the government to significantly increase investment in social spending (see pp. 64–7 for details), a commitment which was only curtailed by the onset of recession in 1993.[3]

Despite the tension provoked by the strike, the PSOE gained a third consecutive general election victory in October 1989 and the PSOE entered the 1990s in confident mood. This confidence was nevertheless misplaced as the party became immersed in a series of corruption allegations which seriously eroded the government's political credibility. Prominent amongst these was the Filesa affair, in which money was channelled illegally to the PSOE via fake consultancy contracts; the Roldán affair, in which the PSOE's appointee as head of the paramilitary *Guardia Civil*, Luis Roldán, amassed a fortune at the state's expense; and most serious of all, the GAL (*Grupos Antiterroristas de Liberación* – Antiterrorist Liberation Groups) affair, in which it emerged that the government had set up death squads tasked with murdering alleged members of the Basque terrorist group ETA between 1983 and 1987.

To add to the party's malaise, the government's economic credibility was simultaneously damaged by the onset of recession. As a consequence of these developments, the unity and discipline which had been such key characteristics of the PSOE throughout the 1980s now began to break down.

To the surprise of most commentators, the PSOE was nevertheless able to pull off a fourth consecutive general election victory in June

1993, albeit whilst losing its overall majority. Dependent on the suppor
of the Catalan nationalist party, *Convergència i Unió* (Convergenc
and Union – CiU) to remain in power, González was forced to cal
fresh elections for March 1996, when the Catalans withdrew thei
support. Although the PSOE went down to defeat at the hands of th
centre-right *Partido Popular* (Popular Party – PP), it did so by th
surprisingly narrow margin of 1.4 per cent of the vote.

1.4 The PSOE in Opposition 1996–2004

Felipe González, who had led the party for over two decades and bee
prime minister for almost fourteen years, resigned as PSOE genera
secretary in June 1997, and was replaced by Joaquín Almunia. Almuni
was nevertheless successfully challenged by Josep Borrell, formerl
public works minster under González, as the party's candidate to face Jos
María Aznar at the next general election due in 2000, only for Borre
to resign from the party leadership in May 1999, when it emerged tha
officials responsible to him when he had held the post of treasury secretar
were facing charges of corruption. Joaquín Almunia therefore returne
to lead the party at the general election called for March 2000.

The most notable aspect of the 2000 election campaign was th
PSOE's ill-fated decision to reach an electoral pact with the communist
dominated *Izquierda Unida* (United Left – IU) on the eve of the poll
Aiming to attract left of centre voters who were otherwise likely t
abstain, the initiative found little favour with the Spanish electorat
overall and the percentage of the vote gained by the PSOE slumpe
from 38 per cent in 1996 to 34 per cent in 2000 and the number o
PSOE deputies in the lower house of parliament, the *Congreso de lo
Diputados*, decreased from 141 to 125, the lowest total since the 197
general election.

Given the scale of the defeat, Almunia immediately resigned, to b
replaced by José Luis Rodríguez Zapatero, who was elected genera
secretary in July 2000. The challenge facing the new leader was con
siderable. Taking over the leadership at a historical low point, he had t
move the party on to a definitive post-González era whilst engineerin
an effective opposition to a Popular Party government whose unity
discipline and unquestioned leadership were reminiscent of the qualitie
displayed by the Socialist Party when it entered office in 1982.

Consecutive general election defeats in 1996 and 2000 had left th
party on the defensive and, perhaps understandably after such a lon

period in office, the party struggled to assert itself as an effective opposition party. One positive outcome from the party's two successive election defeats was that it felt impelled to carry out a thorough self-critique. At its 35th congress in 2000, the party adopted a series of resolutions on the causes and consequences of its two successive general election defeats.[4] Its internal instability, lack of unity and uncertain leadership had all led to a haemorrhage of popular support. Meanwhile, the majority of Spaniards remained satisfied with José María Aznar's PP government, which had taken full advantage of the upturn in the Spanish economy that had been apparent since the mid–1990s. With the capture of an overall parliamentary majority in 2000, the PP's dominance within the country left the socialists in a marginal position. They had become too engrossed in their own internal affairs, losing sight of the needs of the electorate. Questions relating to the renewal of the party's organization and leadership, and the procedures for the selection of party leaders, for instance, were of limited interest to the average Spanish voter. Furthermore, tensions had been caused by the contradictions in the party's efforts to develop a coherent political project for Spain as a whole, whilst simultaneously promoting policies for particular regions of the country.

Insufficient consideration had led to the adoption of confused and contradictory policy positions. The Socialist Party had also been ineffective in conveying to the Spanish electorate the scale of its achievements in office, focusing rather on its failures. People now accepted its welfare achievements as irreversible, and the PP government had been sufficiently prudent to curb the scale of its welfare reforms, in particular limiting further privatization of the health and educations systems. With respect to its electoral base, the party had lost the vital support of the urban middle classes, thereby becoming divorced from the majority sector of Spanish society. Consequently, it increasingly relied on the support of the less educated, low-income sectors of the electorate. Exhausted after its long period in government, it had also lost energy and direction and was poorly focused. It had shown itself singularly ineffective as an opposition force at all levels, from local to national level and did not deserve to be returned to office until it had shown itself to be capable of functioning as an effective opposition party.

Given the scale of these challenges, it was felt that a first step towards a return to office would be a purge of the leadership. The generational shift within the party leadership at the 35th congress to bring this about was notable. The executive committee which emerged from the congress had an average age of just under forty-three – eight year younger than its predecessor. The new general secretary, José Lu Rodríguez Zapatero, was just thirty-nine years old. The new leadershi therefore had the added task of disproving those commentators wh considered that the relative inexperience of those now at the top c the party might further diminish the PSOE's effectiveness.

Ironically, Rodríguez Zapatero's task in opposition was facilitate somewhat by the manner in which Aznar's Popular Party chose t govern once in receipt of an overall majority. Increasingly disincline to continue with the inclusive style which had so marked its first terr in office, Aznar's Popular Party government gave the impression o high-handedness in several policy areas. Most notable amongst thes were the regional autonomy question – where efforts were made t draw a line under the entire process, thereby antagonizing the govern ment's erstwhile allies amongst the nationalist parties during its firs term in office – and foreign affairs, where the traditional EU-oriente policy framework established under González's socialist government wa increasingly replaced by a shrill Atlanticism, culminating in Spain support for the US-led attack on Iraq in March 2003 and the despatcl of three hundred Spanish military personnel to the region after th fall of Baghdad to US forces.

Given the opposition of the overwhelming majority of the populatio to Spanish participation in the war – opinion polls consistently indicate that around 90 per cent of Spaniards were opposed to the war – th PSOE was able to reap political capital from its opposition to th government's Iraq policy. In its manifesto for the 2004 general election the socialists condemned the government's 'unconditional support fo the illegal military intervention in Iraq by the United States and th United Kingdom'[5]. Spanish troops would only remain in Iraq if th United Nations, with the support of the international community was able to ensure the transfer of control over the country back to th Iraqis following free elections.[6]

Whatever the contribution of the PSOE's opposition to the war t the party's recovery, it nevertheless appeared to be insufficient to preven a third consecutive Popular Party victory at the general electio scheduled for 14 March 2004, as the government confidently expecte its relatively successful stewardship of the economy to be rewarde Whilst the al-Qaida terrorist attacks on Madrid three days befor Spaniards went to the polls by no means guaranteed the government defeat, the hapless performance of the Popular Party and its medi mis)management during the period between the attacks and polling day had a fateful impact on the final result. It might be more accurate to suggest that it was the Popular Party which lost the election, rather than the PSOE which won it. In order to recapture the support of the Spanish electorate, which had been left in a state of shock after the terrorist attacks, the PSOE nevertheless had to show itself to be a party capable of government. It is a measure of the progress made by the party under the leadership of Rodríguez Zapatero, that the PSOE was able to achieve this.

Eight years before, the PSOE had left office looking tired, devoid of ideas and seriously tarnished by corruption allegations. It had been led for almost a quarter of a century by a leader, Felipe González, whose very dominance hardly facilitated the efforts of his various successors to reinvent the party. That the party was indeed able to return to office so swiftly was an indication of both the party's resilience and the prudence of its decision to opt for a generational shift within the party leadership.

1.5 The PSOE back in office 2004–present

On the very day he moved into the *Moncloa*, the official residence of Spain's prime minister, Rodríguez Zapatero announced the immediate withdrawal of Spanish troops from Iraq, a pledge which was made good within weeks. With similar haste, Spanish foreign policy went back to the pro-European stance which has long been a feature of the PSOE's foreign policy (see below, section 5). The stalemate on the new EU constitution caused by a dispute over voting rights in the Council of Ministers dating back to the 2000 Nice Treaty was speedily resolved by the new government. The government argued that it was fitting that Spain, which had been so late in boarding the train of European integration, was the first EU member state to vote in favour of the constitution at the referendum held in February 2005.

In the social sphere, the incoming government was also quick to make its mark. Indeed, composition of the incoming government was itself an illustration of the PSOE's embrace of positive discrimination: half of Rodríguez Zapatero's new cabinet was made up of women. Positive discrimination would also be employed to address the imbalance in several occupations, including posts at all levels of government. Rodríguez Zapatero also personally considered his government's intro-duction of legislation aimed at combating domestic violence as one its most important achievements during its early period in office.

Furthermore, a year after gaining office, the government legislated in favour of same-sex marriage, as well as supporting the right of same-sex couples to adopt – despite the protests of the Spanish Catholic Church.

Another notable achievement of the PSOE's first year in office was its decision to legalize the position of many thousands of foreign workers in Spain. The government argued that the country needed immigrant labour, a stance which contrasted considerably with the anti-immigrant stance displayed by several other EU member states.

2. Party Structures and Election Performance

Following the momentous events of 1979, when Felipe Gonzále temporarily resigned from the leadership of the party, the PSOE established itself as a unified, disciplined political party under an undisputed leader. Power was concentrated at the very top of the party For instance, at its congress in 1981, a nine-member permanent commission (dominated by Felipe González and his right-hand man Alfonso Guerra) was established, which was responsible for the day to-day running of the party.[7]

The relatively small size of the party membership and the ample opportunities for patronage during the PSOE's long period in government, enabling (compliant) PSOE sympathizers to be appointed to public office (the establishment of Spain's system of autonomy offered yet more opportunities), further encouraged party discipline.

The PSOE's adoption of a more 'catch-all' electoral strategy bore fruit at the 1982 general election when the party obtained almost half of the vote. Throughout the 1980s, the bulk of support for the party came from workers, whether employed or unemployed, pensioners and housewives, whilst younger urban dwellers were also attracted to the party's progressive image. The PSOE also relied on the votes of employees in a public sector which expanded rapidly under the socialists.

The party's electoral support was well distributed around the country and it attracted voters from across the electoral spectrum, thereby confirming its evolution into a 'catch-all' party. Just one fifth of its votes came from the manual working class, whilst the party gained more votes than any other party in all professional and employee sectors of the population with the exception of small and medium sized entrepreneurs. Furthermore, the proportion of party members

rom professional and white-collar sectors of the community also
emained significant with respect to previous general elections.

With the onset of recession and the many allegations of corruption
aunting the PSOE during the 1990s, the party's discipline, unity and
oherence all suffered. By 1996 support for the PSOE had waned
o such an extent that the party emerged victorious only in Andalusia,
Castilla-La Mancha and Asturias. This electoral reliance on the
ountry's most economically backward regions was mirrored by a
lependence on the least dynamic social groups, particularly the
lderly, who had benefited significantly from the PSOE government's
velfare reforms.

This decline was even more apparent at the 2000 general election.
In a low turnout – barely 70 per cent, compared to 78 per cent four
ears before – the PSOE gained 34 per cent of the vote (125 seats) to
he PP's 44.5 per cent (184 seats). The PSOE nevertheless still gained
ust 3.5 per cent less of the vote than in 1996, indicating that the
arty's electoral *floor* was still quite high, thereby leaving hope for the
uture.

The chief difference between the PSOE's performance in the 2000
eneral election and the 2004 general election was that – given the
articular circumstances of the 2004 general election in the aftermath
f the terrorist attacks on Madrid – the PSOE was able to mobilize
ts supporters far more effectively. Participation was high (77 per
ent), and the PSOE was able to gain thirty-nine seats, giving a total
f 164 seats. Most impressively, the party was able to attract
lmost eleven million votes (three million more than in 2000), a
otal which even surpassed Felipe González's best general election
esult in 1982. Although the PSOE failed to gain an overall majority,
he result was viewed by many as a personal achievement for
Rodríguez Zapatero, who was fighting his first general lection as
arty leader.

. The PSOE and the *Estado de las Autonomías*

n the immediate aftermath of the failed *coup d'état* of February 1981,
he PSOE, whilst in opposition, had offered the UCD government its
upport for the controversial *Ley Orgánica de Armonización del Proceso
Autonómico* (Organic Law on the Harmonization of the Autonomy
Process – LOAPA), which sought to establish that the power of the

Autonomous Communities to legislate in certain areas would be subjec
to the approval of central government. When the constitutional cour
ruled in August 1983 that a significant proportion of the draft law wa
judged to be unconstitutional, the PSOE, now in government, re
considered its entire approach towards the autonomy process.

Its chief task with respect to Spain's Autonomous Communities wa
no less than the rationalization and consolidation of an increasingl
dynamic process of decentralization. Effectively, the PSOE had t
square the circle of minimizing the flexibility of the devolutio
process, whilst simultaneously reinforcing the dominant role of th
central state and responding to the demands of the Autonomou
Communities.[8]

This approach increased the importance of the constitutional court
which had jurisdiction over disputes between central government an
the Autonomous Communities over which competencies were 'exclusive
or 'shared'. The court ruled on 847 cases between 1981 and 1993, th
vast majority emanating from Catalonia and the Basque Country.
The number of cases brought before the constitutional court fe
sharply after 1989, suggesting the establishment of improved levels o
communication between central government and the Autonomou
Communities.[10]

One of the chief sources of dispute was the question of the financin
of the Autonomous Communities. Although article 156 of the consti
tution states that Autonomous Communities should enjoy financia
autonomy, regions were awarded more freedom in the spending o
revenue and in the drawing up of their own budgets, than in levyin
their own taxes or sharing in taxes levied by the state.[11]

With the exception of Navarre and the Basque Country, who are abl
to levy and collect almost all taxes, the Autonomous Communitie
were subject to the *Ley Orgánica de Financiación de las Comunidade
Autónomas* (Organic Law on the Funding of the Autonomou
Communities – LOFCA) approved by parliament in 1980. Under th
terms of the LOFCA, regions received a block grant, dependent o
the cost of carrying out the responsibilities transferred to them. The
were also allowed to retain the revenues from certain specified taxe
and other sources, such as fines, once authorized to do so by the centra
government. Due to the protracted nature of the devolution of power
to the regions, transitional arrangements were put in place betwee
1980 and 1986. Autonomous Communities took on increasing power
and responsibilities thereafter. As a result, the percentage of tota

public spending fell sharply, from a fraction under 90 per cent in 1980 to just below 66 per cent in 1994.[12]

Article 16 of the LOFCA had also provided for the establishment of the *Fondo de Compensación Interterritorial* (Inter-regional Compensation Fund – FCI), and further legislation was introduced in 1984 to reactivate the body.[13] Thereafter, the FCI, which was responsible for a minimum of 30 per cent of total public investment, was intended as a means of addressing the disparities between Spain's regions by providing grants for capital investment. The annual provision for the FCI had grown by 1994 to some 128,845 million pesetas ($1.3 billion or £645 million).[14] Regional disparities nevertheless remain considerable. For example, per capita disposable income in Extremadura was only two thirds that of the Balearic Islands in 1993 and Extremadura's per capita GDP was less than half that of the Balearic Islands.[15]

The five-year period stipulated for the ten Autonomous Communities proceeding towards autonomy via the 'slow track' provided for in article 143 of the constitution came to an end in 1987. Their claims for a similar level of autonomy to that enjoyed by the remaining Autonomous Communities were voiced with increasing vehemence thereafter. Despite some procrastination, the government finally reached a *pacto autonómico* (autonomous pact) with the PP in February 1992, aimed at rationalizing the autonomy process. In exchange for agreeing an overall maximum level of responsibility, or *techo autonómico*, the ten 'slow track' Autonomous Communities assumed thirty-two new areas of responsibility, including responsibility for education and certain social services. A system of *conferencias sectoriales* (sectoral conferences) was also established, aimed at improving communication between the central state and Autonomous Communities, and between the individual Autonomous Communities.

During the PSOE's first decade in office, the autonomy process had therefore made significant, if costly, progress. The debt incurred by the regional and local levels of government rose seven-fold between 1983 and 1993, from 952,900 million pesetas (of which the Autonomous Communities accounted for 163,700 million pesetas) to 6,602,100 million pesetas (the Autonomous Communities accounting for 3,782,400 million pesetas).[16]

Debt-servicing by the Autonomous Communities accounted for 5.2 per cent of nominal GDP at the end of 1994, up from 1 per cent of GDP in 1987. Including the local tier of government, total debt was 9.4 per cent of GDP. The number of people on the payroll of the seventeen Autonomous Communities rose fourteen-fold between 1982 and October 1995 to 621,616, as powers were transferred, and those employed by local government more than doubled to 425,881. The number working for the central government, however, fell by only a quarter to 905,801.[17] It should be noted that in contrast to the transfer of responsibilities for expenditure, income remained largely tied to transfers from the state to meet the cost of providing the services that were transferred.[18] According to one study in 1994, only 14 per cent of the revenue of Spain's regional governments came from taxes and 86 per cent from central government transfers and debt instruments, compared with 28 per cent and 72 per cent respectively in Germany and 46 per cent and 54 per cent in the United States.[19] Indeed, this lack of fiscal co-responsibility has been described as 'a regional politician's dream', albeit one in which central government has been reluctant to cede real power over spending.[20]

Steps made towards devolving government authority from the centre to the regions constrained the state's management of the economy, requiring it to engage in a more consultative process in developing economic policy. Moreover, it added an extra dimension to control over public expenditure. Without doubt, the amount of financial resources available to the Autonomous Communities and the degree of budgetary autonomy enjoyed by them, constituted two significant indicators of their degree of political autonomy.[21]

This expense was particularly problematic given the PSOE government's efforts to meet the Maastricht convergence criteria. The level of debt incurred by regional and local government therefore added to the difficulties brought about by the downturn in the economy during the early 1990s. In this context, the government stalled over the introduction of so-called *corresponsabilidad fiscal* (fiscal co-responsibility), the transfer to the Autonomous Communities of a percentage of income tax receipts. Although the initiative had the advantage of establishing at least a partial link between the raising of revenue and the spending of that revenue by the Autonomous Communities, the government was still concerned about the effect of the measure on the central state's budget deficit.

The loss of the PSOE's overall majority at the general election in June 1993 nevertheless weakened the hand of central government and strengthened that of the Autonomous Communities. Dependent on the support of the Catalan nationalist CiU to remain in power, the PSOE agreed to introduce fiscal co-responsibility within three months of the election. According to the terms of the two-year agreement, the Autonomous Communities would retain and dispose of 15 per cent of their own income tax revenues.[22]

The measure had a relatively modest effect on the central state's finances, representing an additional cost of 9,757 million pesetas in 1995, of which Catalonia accounted for 2,615 million pesetas.[23] Poorer Autonomous Communities nevertheless feared that this development would ultimately be of more benefit to wealthier regions, on account of their greater tax-generating capacity. The initiative nevertheless represented progress as regards making the Autonomous Communities assume responsibilities for both spending *and* collecting taxes, thereby promoting greater budgetary discipline.

During its final term in office (1993–6), the PSOE also sought to transform the upper house of the Spanish parliament, the *Senado* (Senate), into a more genuine *Cámara de representación territorial* (House of Territorial Representation), in accordance with article 69 of the constitution. This gave rise to the possibility that at some time in the future, senators would be elected directly by the regional assemblies and the Senate would be charged with initiating legislation relating to the Autonomous Communities.[24]

The Senate unanimously approved a motion in November 1994 whereby the Autonomous Communities would be allowed to form part of Spain's representation in EU institutions during the second half of 1995, when Spain held the EU presidency.[25] Such developments were controversial given that article 149.1 of the constitution awards the central state exclusive competence over several areas, including foreign and security policy. The Autonomous Communities have nevertheless sought to influence EU decisions both at the domestic and EU level, using formal, as well as informal, channels.[26]

Tensions over the question of regional autonomy were neutralized somewhat during the Popular Party's first term in office (1996–2000) due to the Aznar government's dependence on the parliamentary support of nationalist parties. This consensual approach contrasted sharply with the more confrontational stance which Aznar adopted once he was in receipt of an overall majority between 2000 and 2004. The PSOE's response in opposition was to advocate strengthening and extending the *State of the Autonomies* and the party now clearly sought to work towards a federalist future for Spain, albeit within the framework of the 1978 constitution. Whereas the Popular Party government essentially sought to draw a line under the entire process from

2000, the PSOE, now under the leadership of José Luis Rodríguez Zapatero, made clear its belief that the passage of time had rendered necessary further revision of the autonomy statutes, particularly in Catalonia, Andalusia and the Basque Country.

This stance contributed towards the PSOE being able – thanks to an alliance with the leftist *Esquerra Republicana de Catalunya* (Catalan Republican Left – ERC) – to put an end to 23 years of centre-right *Convergència i Unió* (Convergence and Union – CiU) hegemony within the region, enabling the socialist Pasqual Maragall to become president of the region in December 2003. ERC would again play a key role three months later when it offered its parliamentary support to Rodríguez Zapatero following the PSOE's slender general election victory.

Following its general election victory in March 2004, the PSOE set about establishing an annual 'Presidents' Conference', which would serve as a forum for cooperation between central government and the leaders of Spain's seventeen Autonomous Communities. Significantly, the body held its first meeting at the Senate in Madrid in October 2004, thereby underlining the PSOE's desire to convert the Spanish upper house into an institution more closely linked to the regional autonomy process.

However, whereas progress was made on reforming several autonomy statutes, Rodríguez Zapatero's government rejected outright the 'Ibarretxe Plan', originally put forward in 2002 by the Basque nationalist president of the Basque region, Juan José Ibarretxe. The plan, proposing a model of free association for the Basque nation within the Spanish state (influenced by the 'sovereignty association' model advocated by Quebec nationalists in their relationship with the rest of Canada), was narrowly approved by the Basque parliament in December 2004, but heavily defeated when put to the vote in the Congress of Deputies in Madrid several weeks later.

It can be concluded that a process of socialization and, particularly after 1992, realpolitik, informed the PSOE government's attitude towards the decentralization of power. Even before the party entered office in 1982, it had played a key role in the elaboration of legislation, the LOAPA, which would have effectively curtailed the autonomy process, and possibly destabilized the relationship between the central state and the regions. The support for the PSOE must be viewed in the context of the sensitivity of the regional question following the *coup d'état* of February 1981. When the LOAPA was ruled to be unconstitutional, the PSOE rejected the adoption of a 'broad brush' approach to decentralization in favour of negotiation with each individual Autonomous Community. Whilst this approach had the disadvantage of many disputes between the central state and the regions having to be settled by the constitutional court, the system had become sufficiently consolidated by the end of the 1980s for the government to consider a further expansion of the process. Just as the PSOE had been able to reach agreement with the UCD government on the autonomy question before reaching office, it again showed its preference for a bi-partisan approach on this sensitive question by reaching a deal with the main opposition party, the PP, on further extending the autonomy process in 1992. The party's remaining period in office was notable for the increase in the bargaining power of the regions, particularly Catalonia, with respect to the central government. This period, therefore, paradoxically witnessed the transfer of further financial powers to the regions at the very time when the chief concern of the central state was to rein in public spending in order for Spain to qualify for economic and monetary union.

The Autonomous Communities also forged a key role in the allocation and distribution of EU structural funds and the sectoral conferences provided the Autonomous Communities with some say with respect to Spain's EU policy. By the end of the PSOE's period in office in 1996, it was apparent that a process was emerging whereby the nation state was being by-passed as direct links became established between the EU and the regions.[27] Back in government in 2004, the PSOE set about institutionalizing the participation of the autonomous regions in Spain's relations with the European Union. Rodríguez Zapatero nevertheless showed himself to be uncompromising with respect to any initiative – such as the Ibarretxe Plan – which appeared to go beyond the framework of the 1978 constitution.

4. PSOE Activities in the Autonomous Communities

The PSOE has granted considerable autonomy to its regional branches, established throughout Spain's Autonomous Communities. For example, the Catalan branch of the PSOE, the Partit dels Socialistes de Catalunya (PSC-PSOE), whilst being organically linked to the Madrid-based PSOE according to the terms of a Unity protocol agreed in 1978, has full sovereignty within Catalonia.[28] The PSC–PSOE has even defied its own Madrid leadership by proposing that Spain should be turned into a federation – the traditional stance of Catalan regionalism.[2] Only after the PSOE's defeat at the 1996 general election did the PSOE officially advocate federalism.

As Richard Gillespie has noted, conflict within the party's regional federations has rarely been about ideology and almost always about power, whilst regional leaders have in the past often been frustrated at their relative lack of weight in the party nationally.[30] Nevertheless, as a result of the party's decline during the 1990s, those party 'barons' still capable of winning in their respective autonomous regions emerged as brokers of considerable power within the national party. For example José Bono, president of the Castilla-La Mancha Autonomous Community, was only narrowly beaten by Zapatero for the post of general secretary in July 2000. Manuel Chaves, president of the Andalusian *Junta*, and Juan Carlos Rodríguez Ibarra, his counterpart in Extremadura retain considerable influence within the PSOE.

The socialist presidents of the Autonomous Communities and the PSOE Federal Executive Committee released a political declaration setting out several proposals aimed at improving the relationship between the Autonomous Communities and central government in Madrid in November 2000.[31] These included:

- regular meetings between the prime minister and presidents of the Autonomous Communities gathered at the Conference of Autonomous Community Presidents to discuss national issues;
- the reform of the Senate so as to convert the upper house of parliament into an effective forum for the exchange of views both between the different governments of the Autonomous Communities, and between the autonomous governments and national government;
- the establishment of multilateral fora to address questions which affect particular autonomous regions, for example the water shortage;
- simplifying the system for financing the Autonomous Communities by initiating negotiations between representatives of the Autonomous Communities and central government within a reformed Senate;
- encouraging the greater participation of the Autonomous Communities in European Union affairs; the newly reformed Senate would rule on when representatives of the Autonomous Communities would form part of Spanish delegations to the EU

Progress has been made in implementing a good proportion of these measures since the PSOE's general election victory in March 2004. The party's attitude towards the Autonomous Communities has therefore become less 'centralist' over time, as the party has advocated a shift in the balance of power between central government and the Autonomous Communities in favour of the latter. A more overtly federal system is now firmly on the current PSOE government's political agenda.

Figure 2.1: Electoral Performance of the PSOE in Basque Autonomous Community (Regional) Elections 1980–2001

Year	1980	1984	1986	1990	1994	1998	2001	2005
Seats	9	19	19	16	12	14	13	18
% of vote	8.4	15.6	15.2	12	10	12	14	22.6
No. of votes	130,221	247,786	252,233	202,736	174,682	218,607	253,195	272.429

Sources: *www.ehe.es/spvweb/paginas/resultados/tablas* and
www.elpais.es/comunes/2005/elecciones vascas/index.html

Figure 2.2: Electoral Performance of the PSOE in Catalan Autonomous Community (Regional) Elections 1980–2003

Year	1980	1984	1988	1992	1995	1999	2003
Seats	33	41	42	40	34	50	42
% of vote	22.4	30.1	29.8	27.5	24.8	37.9	31.2
No. of votes	608,609	865,447	800,999	726,099	797,422	1,177,777	1,026,030

Sources: *www.diba.es/icps/castella/resultats.htm* and
www.elmundo.es/especiales/2003/11/catalunya/elecciones/catalunya.html2004

Figure 2.3: Electoral Performance of the PSOE in Galician Autonomous Community (Regional) Elections 1981–2001

Year	1981	1985	1989	1993	1997	2001
Seats	16	22	28	19	13	17
% of vote	19.2	28.3	32.4	23.6	19.4	21.7
No. of votes	193,456	361,946	433,256	396,415	310,508	334,819

Sources: *www.eleweb.net/castellano/elecciones.html* and
www.diba.es/icps/working_papers/docs/Wp_i_57.pdf, Anuario El País 1998, p 88, Anuario El País 2002, p 113

5. The PSOE and Europe

The PSOE has deep roots in the western European social democratic tradition and is generally considered to be the most 'European' of Spain's statewide political parties. European integration provided the party with a major framework for policy throughout its period in office between 1982 and 1996. The party's identification with 'Europe' was in line with the beliefs of prominent 'Europeanizers' within the PSOE leadership throughout the party's long history, such as Fernando de los Ríos and Julián Besteiro. For over a century, therefore, the party has viewed 'Europe' as being the solution to Spain's chronic historical problems of economic backwardness, authoritarianism and international isolation.

When the PSOE entered office in 1982, the party's ambitious aim was to consolidate Spain's recently established democracy and to transform the country in such a way as to gain a place amongst Europe's leading group of countries. With its historical identification with 'Europe' as a force for democratization, peace and progress, allied to its excellent links to European social democratic sister parties, particularly Germany's SPD, the PSOE considered itself to be uniquely equipped for this task

Foremost amongst the areas of policy most directly influenced by Spain's membership of the European Union were economic policy and foreign and security policy. With respect to the economy, the PSOE aimed to transform Spain's economy into an open, modern and integrated economy capable of attracting investment and of competing internationally. Indeed, there could be no definitive consolidation of Spanish democracy until the economy had been stabilized.

More than any other single factor, integration provided the PSOE with the framework for its economic policy throughout its entire period in office:

- its first term in office between 1982 and 1986 was geared towards preparing the economy for the competitive rigours of EC membership by means of a painful industrial restructuring process, accompanied by a tough fiscal policy and cuts in social spending;
- between 1986 and 1991 the economy was rapidly opened up in accordance with the terms of the EC Accession Treaty and the simultaneous Single European Act, a period most notable for an exceptional period of investment-driven economic growth;

• and from 1992 to 1996, its economic policy was dominated by the PSOE government's efforts to meet the Maastricht convergence criteria for economic and monetary union in the context of serious recession.

The case of Spain is notable for the consensus in favour of European membership and integration throughout the Spanish population and across the political spectrum and the comparative lack of debate within Spanish society on the question of European integration. With Spain enjoying the highest levels of economic growth in the EC between 1986 and 1990, there was general agreement that EC membership had an overwhelmingly positive influence on Spanish economic development. Only after 1992, a full decade after the PSOE entered office, did any genuine debate on European integration emerge as the Spanish economy experienced its deepest recession in decades and, even then debate was sporadic. The only national Spanish political party to mount an effective criticism of the economic and monetary union project, the IU (criticism was confined to EMU, rather than Spain's membership of the European Union per se), discovered that such a stance hardly proved a vote-winner. In the Spanish context, criticism of the European 'project' virtually meant electoral suicide.

The crisis within the Exchange Rate Mechanism (ERM) in September 1992 forced the government into a major reappraisal of monetary policy, including a devaluation of the peseta by 5 per cent. Whilst Spain had not been the only country obliged by its membership of the ERM to maintain interest rates at a level inconsistent with the requirements of the domestic economy, the PSOE government nevertheless refused to follow the example of the UK and Italy by withdrawing the peseta from the discredited system, despite successive devaluations over the following months. On the contrary, the socialists viewed any such withdrawal as a betrayal of their commitment to European integration. They had identified so greatly with the European 'project' that, in effect, political considerations – the need to keep faith with the 'project' – outweighed economic concerns.

The economic downturn led the PSOE government to place greater emphasis on economic and social cohesion. As the chief advocate for the establishment of the new Cohesion Fund at the December 1992 Edinburgh Council meeting, Felipe González successfully obtained for Spain over half of the 15 billion ecus (at 1992 prices) made available to the Fund, the balance going to Portugal (18 per cent), Greece (18 per cent) and Ireland (9 per cent). It was also agreed at Edinburgh to double the financial resources available to the structural funds, of which Spain also obtained the lion's share: 34,443 million ecus between 1994–9, over half as much again as the second largest recipient, Germany, which received 21,724 million ecus. This sum was equivalent to 1.4 per cent of Spain's GDP during the period. In 1996, the year the PSOE left office, Spain was the largest net recipient of EU transfers, obtaining one third of resources. In all, Spain obtained 27 per cent of the EU's total structural resources (structural fund and cohesion fund combined) between 1994 and 1999.

In an attempt to meet the Maastricht convergence criteria, the government adopted privatization to improve the public finances. Although the PSOE government had never had an official privatization programme, it had been quite active in totally or partially selling off state-owned companies. The urgency imposed by the government's attempt to meet the Maastricht convergence criteria witnessed a particular intensification of stock market flotations of public companies during the PSOE's final years in office.

Although the Spanish economy was undoubtedly transformed under the PSOE and the country was able to enjoy a protracted period of economic boom in the late 1980s, many problems remained when the PSOE left office in 1996. These included:

- an above EU average unemp•oyment rate (unemployment never fell below 16 per cent throughout the PSOE's entire period in office);
- over-dependence on foreign investment;
- an above-average foreign penetration of the economy;
- a failure to meet the Maastricht convergence criteria (which were nevertheless met by the PSOE's PP successors in government).

Despite this mixed success, the PSOE had nevertheless been able to build a welfare state virtually from scratch and transform the country's infrastructure. Indeed, whilst many commentators have made much of what they view as the 'neo-liberal' elements of the PSOE's economic policies, less emphasis has been placed on the PSOE's record with regard to the social distribution of resources and the improvement of Spain's infrastructure. The PSOE's record of public investment in health, education, pensions, unemployment benefits and other social provision, as well as infrastructure, was considerable, particularly during its third term in office (1989–93), as the economic boom period provided the resources for increased levels of public investment. This omission is serious since no rigorous explanation of the PSOE's electoral strength over the years can ignore the party's achievements in these areas.

Six million Spaniards had no access to public health care in 1982. By the early 1990s, the entire population had access to free health care. Minimum pension rights were similarly extended to the entire population. The amount spent on unemployment benefits more than doubled in terms of percentage of GDP to 4.8 per cent of GDP between 1983 and 1994.[32] Spending on education also increased five-fold during the decade 1982–92. Total public sector spending by 1995, the PSOE's last full year in office, was almost 50 per cent of GDP, of which outlays on the welfare state (pensions, unemployment benefits, health, education, housing and other social services) accounted for around half, in line with the EU average.[33]

Capital spending also rose significantly in the late 1980s and early 1990s. The Economist Intelligence Unit has noted, 'Spain in the mid-1980s still had an infrastructure more appropriate to a developing country than to Europe's fastest growing economy'.[34] The PSOE's record in investment in infrastructure thereafter was impressive and public spending on roads, railways, ports and airports, oil and gas pipelines, communications and hydraulic projects almost tripled between 1986 and 1991.

By 1992, the deteriorating economic situation led to the first year-on-year decrease in the amount spent on public works programmes since 1984 and in 1995 the government formally dropped the spending commitment which it had made just three years before. With gaps opening up in the public finances, the government chose to cut back on public works programmes rather than cut deeper into the even more politically sensitive social security budget.

The commitment of public resources to improve Spain's welfare and infrastructure was presented by the PSOE as a further aspect of Spain's 'modernization', in the sense of Spain seeking to catch up with its fellow European member states. To this extent, the PSOE chose to portray Spain's compliance with the economic demands of the European 'project' and public spending on welfare and infrastructure as two sides of the same 'modernization' coin. The PSOE's 'modernization' project for Spain was not, after all, solely concerned with economic imperatives, although macroeconomic stability was undoubtedly the chief foundation and prerequisite of that project.

Remaining at the heart of the European project and providing levels of social protection and infrastructure similar to those in Europe's leading countries were both key aspects of 'Europeanization'. The European 'project' therefore served the PSOE as a point of reference as well as providing it with impeccable political justification for both potentially unpopular policy decisions, such as the PSOE government's efforts to meet the Maastricht convergence criteria, as well as for policies likely to find more favour with the public, such as increased spending on welfare and infrastructure. In essence, the market could be embraced without totally restricting the PSOE's capacity to lay the foundations of a modern welfare state.

In the context of the PSOE's efforts to maintain Spain at the forefront of the European integration 'project', particularly inclusion in economic and monetary union, the dilemma of balancing the demands of market efficiency and social cohesion was acute. The tension between the liberal economic framework provided by the European 'project', with its overriding emphasis on price stability, and the more traditionally social democratic emphasis on public investment in welfare and infrastructure, therefore, became more apparent towards the end of the party's period in office.

Just as with economic policy, European integration had a decisive influence on the PSOE's Spanish foreign and security policy orientations. With respect to foreign policy, EU membership offered the PSOE the opportunity of injecting substance into Spain's relationship with the two traditional areas of Spanish foreign policy interest, the Mediterranean and Latin America. Despite the Franco regime's bombast, its 'special relationship' with both areas contained little of real substance and the relative neglect of foreign affairs by UCD governments between 1977 and 1982 had done little to change this state of affairs. Having secured Spain's membership of the EC, the PSOE sought to utilize its membership to elaborate a more realistic and mutually beneficial relationship with the two regions. Whilst the PSOE obtained only modest success with regard to Latin America, it did manage to establish Spain as a key player in the elaboration of the EU's policy in the Mediterranean.

The most pressing security policy question facing the PSOE concerned the country's membership of NATO, which had been hastily secured by the previous UCD government in May 1982. As the PSOE moved towards securing entry into the EC, it was forced to reassess its policy of opposition to Spain's membership of NATO, as it became convinced of the inextricable link between Spain's membership of the two organizations. Only by gaining entry into the EC and accepting the country's responsibilities within NATO, could the PSOE consign to history Spain's international isolation. Similarly, NATO membership offered a means of improving Spain's strained relationship with the United States. The PSOE's traumatic experience of not just performing a volte-face on the issue, but obtaining the endorsement of the public for its change of stance in the referendum of March 1986, led to tensions within Spanish society, and indeed within the PSOE itself, which were eventually defused with the passage of time. The party's embracing of NATO did not prevent the PSOE from establishing itself as one of the EU member countries most in favour of a more pronounced European foreign and security policy identity. Initiatives such as the Common Foreign and Security Policy (CFSP) contained in the Maastricht Treaty were fully supported by the PSOE. As Barbé has concluded, 'the common foreign policy (as well as European security/defence) was an important tool in the process of Europeanization initiated by the Socialist government with all that it entailed'.[35]

With Spain's entry into the Western European Union (WEU) in 1988, the PSOE had brought the country's security arrangements in line with EU norms, enabling Spain to participate fully in the framework of European security. The party sought to present its interest in the development of a European security policy as a logical consequence of the country's integration into the EC and the European security system. Despite the PSOE's interest in a more pronounced EU security identity, it was careful not to propose the WEU/EU as an alternative to NATO, preferring, rather, to stress their complementary character.

It is nevertheless worth noting that the PSOE government chose to present Spain's controversial involvement in the Gulf War in terms of its European security obligations, a strategy viewed as being the best means of retaining the support of a sceptical public unaccustomed to Spanish participation in military action abroad. The wider process of European integration therefore framed the Spanish prime minister's analysis of the Gulf War.[36]

In its policy towards the two traditional areas of Spanish foreign policy concern, the Mediterranean and Latin America, the PSOE's main hypothesis was that Spanish national interest could best be defended by presenting those interests as being in harmony with the interests of the EU as a whole. By 1996, the PSOE had, without doubt, consolidated the country's status as a key player in the EU's relations with the Mediterranean. The success of the Euro Mediterranean Conference in November 1995 during Spain's presidency of the EU was an indication of Spain's growing influence as regards the development of EU policy towards the region. The PSOE was aided in this achievement by the existence of an existing Mediterranean lobby amongst EU member states and the party was able to utilize its membership of the EU to develop a more effective policy towards the region.

The PSOE's efforts to promote a comparable degree of EU engagement in Latin America were thwarted by the EU's recognition that the region belonged within the US sphere of influence. Although there was no significant change in the EU's policy towards the region, Spain was able to establish a significant investment profile in the region during the 1990s. Indeed, Spain's success as an investor poses the question as to whether an increased EU interest in the region would be detrimental to Spanish national interests.

Returned to office in 2004, the PSOE distanced itself from the previous government's Atlanticism and again emphasized what it viewed as being the three priority areas of Spanish foreign policy: the European Union, the Mediterranean and Latin America. As we have seen above, the current PSOE government has been able to reach an agreement on voting rights in the Council of Ministers, thereby unblocking the deadlock on the European constitution. The Spanish people's approval of the constitution in February 2005 was an indication that the EU had once again become the central focus of Spanish foreign policy concern, as it had previously been under the PSOE government led by Felipe González between 1982 and 1996.

Conclusion

After almost fourteen years in power, the PSOE found it difficult to regenerate itself as an effective opposition force and as a credible candidate for a return to office. Towards the end of his long period as party leader, Felipe González expressed the view that he was unsure as to whether his continued leadership of the party constituted more of a hindrance than a help to the PSOE. Certainly, the question of leadership proved to be the party's main problem in recent years, as shown by the bewildering succession of party leaders who sought to fill González's shoes after 1997.

The corruption allegations, which did so much to blemish the PSOE's many fine achievements in government, particularly with respect to economic modernization and the devolution of power to Spain's regions, continued to hamper the party's rehabilitation in the minds of many Spaniards. With the election of José Luis Rodríguez Zapatero as PSOE general secretary in 2000, the party opted to distance itself from its recent past by promoting a younger generation of party leaders.

This decision appeared to be an astute move in the aftermath of the shock caused by the terrorist attacks of 11 March 2004, as the Spanish people voted the PSOE, now fronted by a fresh, post-González generation of leaders, back into office. Moreover, the party's recovery under Rodríguez Zapatero illustrated its resilience, powers of renewal and capacity to bounce back, qualities which the party has been notable for since its foundation a century and a quarter ago.

Notes

[1]   Paul Heywood, *Marxism and the Failure of Organised Socialism in Spain* (Cambridge: Cambridge University Press, 1990), pp. 1–24.

[2]   For the disintegration of the UCD, see Jonathan Hopkin, *Party Formation and Democratic Transition in Spain* (Basingstoke: Macmillan, 1999).

[3]   'Entrevista a Joaquín Almunia', *Leviatán*, No. 68, 1998, 26.

[4]   PSOE, *Resoluciones del 35 Congreso*, 2000.

[5]   PSOE, *Merecemos una España mejor. Programa Electoral. Elecciones Generales 2004*, p. 13.

[6]   Ibid, p. 24.

[7]   Paul Heywood, 'Change within Continuity: The Spanish Socialist Workers' Party (PSOE)', Paper prepared for *ECPR* workshop: 'Different rates and types of change in political parties: from adaptation to transformation', Madrid, 17–22 April 1994, p. 9.

[8]   John L. Hollyman 'The Tortuous Road to Regional Autonomy in Spain', *Journal of the Association for Contemporary Iberian Studies*, 8, 1, (1995), 18.

[9]   John Gibbons, *Spanish Politics Today* (Manchester: Manchester University Press, 1999), p. 21.

[10] Paul Heywood, *The Government and Politics of Spain* (Basingstoke: Macmillan, 1995), pp. 147–9.

[11] Michael T. Newton with Peter J. Donaghy, *Institutions of Modern Spain* (Cambridge: Cambridge University Press, 1997), p. 127.

[12] Newton with Donaghy, p. 126.

[13] Juan Manuel Eguiagaray, 'El Estado Autonómico', in Alfonso Guerra and José Félix Tezanos (eds) *La década del cambio* (Madrid: Sistema, 1992), pp. 334–5.

[14] John Hooper, *The New Spaniards* (London: Penguin, 1995), p. 430.

[15] William Chislett, *Spain: at a turning point* (Madrid: Banco Central Hispano, 1994), p. 137.

[16] José Barea Tejeiro, 'El sector público español ante la integración europea' in Alcaide, Julio et al., *Problemas Económicos Españoles en la Década de los 90* (Barcelona: Círculo de Lectores, 1995) pp. 262–3.

[17] William Chislett, *Spain 1996: The Central Hispano Handbook* (Madrid: Banco Central Hispano, 1996), p. 130.

[18] Keith Salmon, 'The Spanish Economy: From the Single Market to EMU' in Richard Gillespie and Richard Youngs (eds), *Spain: the European and International Challenges* (London: Frank Cass, 2001), pp. 35–36.

[19] William Chislett, *Spain: at a turning point* (Madrid: Banco Central Hispano, 1994), p. 136.

[20] William Chislett, *Spain 1996: The Central Hispano Handbook* (Madrid: Banco Central Hispano, 1996), p. 130.

[21] Francesc Morata, 'El Estado de las Autonomías' in Manuel Alcántara and Antonia Martínez (eds), *Política y Gobierno en España* (Valencia: Tirant lo Blanch, 1997), p. 129.

[22] This figure was doubled to 30 per cent following the *Partido Popular*'s general election victory in March 1996. The narrowness of the victory meant that the *Partido Popular* government, just like its PSOE predecessor, was dependent on the support of the nationalists and regionalists to remain in power. It is worth noting that when the Catalan nationalists supported the Socialists in government, the opposition *Partido Popular* opposed further decentralization measures, accusing the PSOE of making excessive concessions to the Catalans at the expense of the other regions. When the Catalans supported the *Partido Popular* government after the 1996 general election, the PSOE in opposition advanced similar criticism (See Josep M. Colomer, 'The Spanish 'State of Autonomies': Non-Institutional Federalism', in Paul Heywood (ed.), *Politics and Policy in Democratic Spain* (London: Frank Cass, 1999), p. 49.

[23] Casimiro García-Abadillo, *El Balance: luces y sombras de la España del PSOE* (Madrid: Temas de Hoy, 1997), p. 72.

[24] Newton with Donaghy, *Institutions of Modern Spain*, p. 143.

[25] Audrey Brassloff, 'Spain's Centre and Periphery: Is the Tail Wagging the Dog?', paper presented at the Annual Conference of the *Association for Contemporary Iberian Studies*, Keele University, 10–12 September 1996, p. 7.

[26] Francesc Morata, 'Spain' in Rometsch, Dietrich and Wessels, Wolfgang (eds), *The European Union and member states: towards institutional fusion* (Manchester: Manchester University Press, 1996), p. 145.

[27] Paul Heywood, 'Power Diffusion or Concentration? In Search of the Spanish Policy Process' in Paul Heywood (ed.), *Politics and Policy in Democratic Spain*, p. 117.

[28] Paul Heywood, *The Government and Politics of Spain*, pp. 208–9.

[29] Christopher Ross, *Spain 1812–1996* (London: Arnold, 2000), p. 150.

[30] Richard Gillespie, 'The resurgence of factionalism in the Spanish Socialist Workers' Party' in David S. Bell and Eric Shaw (eds), *Conflict and Cohesion in Western European Social Democratic Parties* (London: Pinter,1994), p 59.

[31] Available at *www.psoe.es/NuevasPoliticas-NuevosTiempos/Nuestras Politicas/ Autonomias/ Politica*, accessed 15 January 2001.

[32] William Chislett, *Spain 1996: The Central Hispano Handbook*, p. 28.

[33] William Chislett, *Spain 1996: The Central Hispano Handbook*, p. 27.

[34] Economist Intelligence Unit, 'Spain: Country Profile 1995–96' (London: Economist Intelligence Unit, 1995) p. 21.

[35] Esther Barbé, 'European Political Cooperation: The upgrading of Spanish foreign policy' in Richard Gillespie, Fernando Rodrigo and Jonathan Story (eds), *Democratic Spain: reshaping external relations in a changing world* (London: Routledge, 1995), p. 119.

[36] Michael P. Marks with Susannah Verney, 'Influence and Institutions: EU Relations with Spain and Greece', Paper presented at the Annual Meeting of the *American Political Science Association*, Chicago, August 31–September 3 1995, p. 14.

3

Political Parties in Catalonia

JOHN ETHERINGTON AND ANA-MAR FERNÁNDEZ

Historical Background

Catalonia is one of the historic nationalities of Spain with its own history, language and culture, all of which constitute the elements that form the basis of a distinct Catalan national identity. At the same time, it is one of the principal economic motors of Spain, having enjoyed an early and extensive industrialization that has framed the context for much of its subsequent socio-economic development. For over a century, politics in Catalonia have revolved around two political cleavages. On the one hand, there is the 'national question' or how Catalonia's national identity should be articulated politically in relation to the Spanish state. On the other hand, there is the class conflict between labour and capital that gives rise to the traditional left-right political cleavage. While the Catalan party system shares many of the features of state-level politics in terms of the left–right dimension, the national question has also been of key importance, and, as a result, there are exclusively Catalan nationalist parties with no real links with other parties at the state level. This allows us to talk of a distinct system of political parties in Catalonia.

This chapter will analyse the main political parties in Catalonia: the nationalist *Convergència i Unió* (CiU), a federation made up of two parties, the *Convergència Democràtica de Catalunya* (CDC) and the *Unió Democràtica de Catalunya* (UDC) and the nationalist *Esquerra Republicana de Catalunya* (ERC); the Catalan branches of the Spanish state-level parties: the *Partit dels Socialistes de Catalunya-Partido Socialista Obrero Español* (PSC-PSOE) and the *Partido Popular de Catalunya* (PPC); and *Iniciativa-Els Verds* (IC-V). The *Partido Popular* (PP), however, will only be studied where substantial differences exist with the PP at the Spanish level, given the lack of autonomy that the party has in Catalonia. Having analysed the parties, the overall conclusions will seek to offer an up-to-date vision of each of the parties considered here and of current party politics in Catalonia, with suggestions as to what the future may hold.

Convergència i Unió (CiU)

Introduction and Historical Background

The CiU is a centre-right nationalist federation that emerged with the transition to democracy, and consists of two parties: the *Convergència Democràtica de Catalunya* (CDC), which is the dominant partner, and the *Unió Democràtica de Catalunya* (UDC). Of all the political forces within Catalonia the CiU and its erstwhile leader, Jordi Pujol, have left perhaps the deepest mark on Catalan and Spanish politics in the post-Franco era. Against almost all predictions, the CiU won the first regional elections in Catalonia in 1980, consequently forming the government of the *Generalitat de Catalunya*, a position that would only be lost at the elections of 2003. The *Generalitat* has provided the CiU with a key platform from which to project their political image not only in Catalonia, but also throughout the rest of Spain and, indeed, Europe. Despite never having been the most voted-for party at general elections in Catalonia, the CiU became the key element that guaranteed the political stability of Spain, allowing first the *Partido Socialista Obrero Español* (PSOE) between 1993 and 1996, and then the PP between 1996 and 2000, to govern as a minority with the parliamentary support of the CiU.

The CDC and UDC joined forces in 1978 as a formal coalition, in what was seen at the time as a marriage of convenience. However, despite differences over ideology and above all over representation in the joint electoral lists, the marriage has very much endured, and has established itself as a centre-right nationalist political option with a broad popular appeal. In 2001, the CDC and UDC strengthened their ties, and the CiU went from being a coalition of the two parties to being a federation. While the issue of a fully-fledged merger between the two parties forms part of the political landscape in Catalonia, the current arrangement looks set to continue for the foreseeable future.

For its part, the CDC emerged in 1974 out of the merger of several nationalist, centrist groups, even including social democratic political groups opposed to Francoism. The latter included Pujol's, *El Grup d'Acció al Servei de Catalunya*, (Action Group at the Service of Catalonia) and the UDC itself, which split from the CDC in 1976 to later return in 1978 as a partner in the CiU coalition. From the beginning, Jordi Pujol emerged as the driving force of the party, and the CDC policies very much reflected his desire to create a modern, moderate, nationalist political option,[1] all of which distinguish the CDC from both traditional Catalan nationalist movements and also from other political parties with longer political traditions, such as its coalition partner, the UDC.

The UDC was founded in 1931, the same year as the declaration of the Second Republic. From the beginning the UDC displayed a clearly Christian democrat ideology and a strong commitment to *catalanisme*, political demands made in the name of the Catalan people. During the Franco dictatorship, between 1939 and 1975, the UDC was forced underground, where it maintained its opposition to Franco. In the first free general elections, the UDC did not run with the CDC, but instead ran with two other Christian democrat groups that maintained links with similar groups throughout the rest of the Spanish state,[2] a position which has been a recurrent feature of the UDC until the present day. The poor results obtained – just two seats in the Madrid *Cortes* – led to a fierce debate within the party between the centre-left, pro-Catalan nationalist wing and those who supported the construction of a broad-based centre political group with Suárez's *Unión de Centro Democrático* (UCD) in Catalonia. The former won this debate which led to the latter's leaving the party. From that moment on, the way was open for the formation of the coalition with Pujol's CDC.

1. Party Structure and Membership

The CDC is organized on territorial and sectoral lines, with local and sectoral groups at the bottom of a pyramidal structure grouped together in five territorial federations. At the top of the pyramid, the national, Catalan level, the party has two legislative bodies, the National Council and the National Congress, in addition to the National Executive Committee. The National Council meets every two months and is made up of representatives of the territorial federations and of the sectoral groups, and of members of the various parliaments (European, Catalan and Spanish). The National Council chooses the National Executive Committee, with the exception of the president, the general

ecretary and the secretary of organization, all of whom are directly
elected by the Congress. Thus, while it is the Congress that must approve
he overall direction of the party, the real legislative power lies with the
National Council.

Beyond the formal structure of the party, perhaps three points can
be made:

. Traditionally Jordi Pujol as founder member of the party has
  played a dominant role in the taking of major decisions. His
  semi-retirement from active politics (although he remains party
  president) raises the question of how the party might restructure
  the leadership in order to take into account a greater plurality of
  input into decision making.
. The relative independence of the members of the various
  parliaments allows them to exercise influence over the direction
  of the party.
. While the above two features might lead us to conclude that
  CDC is typically a party of cadres, membership levels, as we
  shall see below, are more in line with a mass party. Indeed, from
  the beginning, the will has existed to go beyond the status of a
  mere political party and become a movement which is not only
  capable of dominating the political institutions but is also able to
  penetrate civil society in order to influence society as a whole.[3]

The party structure of the UDC is, today, very similar to that of the
CDC, with the real executive power being concentrated at the top
level of the party, with 'specialized groups' that include the principal
leaders of the party providing much of the ideological direction.
However, while the party today is a fully professionalized and efficient
electoral machine, this has not always been the case. During the
transition period from Francoism, the UDC was considered to be one
of the most democratic political formations in Catalonia, with a high
degree of grass-roots input and control achieved through mechanisms
such as annual party conferences.[4]

Membership of the CDC has grown from just over a hundred
members at the party's founding assembly in 1974, to the present figure
of 26,000,[5] which to some extent may be attributed to the party's control
of the Autonomous Community, and which has enabled it to become
established in Catalan society.[6] From what was originally an urban
party concentrated in Barcelona, the CDC has spread to all parts of

Catalonia, both rural and urban, including the provinces of Tarragona and Lleida where until the late 1980s the CDC had encountered difficulties in becoming established. The CDC membership is predominantly male, middle-class, well educated, and Catholic church-going.[7]

The UDC's membership is slightly lower, increasing from just over 2,000 in 1980 to the present figure of almost 18,000 according to party sources, and is evenly distributed throughout Catalonia; it is predominantly male (67 per cent), with almost 75 per cent aged between eighteen and fifty.

2. Ideology

Today, the CDC stands out as a pragmatic centre-centre-right moderate nationalist party 'that seeks to be the meeting point of different ideological positions with nationalism as the main point of union and identity. It is, thus, a party of 'convergence' which has laid down its roots in Catalan civil society in order to develop its nationalist political project'.[8] The party has shifted from its initial position of proximity to social democracy to the point where most voters position the party at the centre or centre-right of the left–right political spectrum. While different sectors exist within the party, Jordi Pujol's ability to combine nationalist discourse with political pragmatism has been the key influence over the party's political activity. Nationalism for Pujol entails the defence of Catalan national identity that, to some extent, exists independently of the individual members of the community. This 'pure nationalism without ideological justification' reflects the Christian roots of this ideology and gives it a certain proximity to the conservative *Catalanism* of the nineteenth and early twentieth century'.[9] Catalan national identity serves as the framework within which efforts are made to undertake a process of socio-economic modernization of the country.

Despite the social democratic origins of at least part of the party the CDC has, over the years, increasingly incorporated a neo-liberal economic approach into its political discourse, due to the perceived need to integrate Catalonia into the European and international markets. However, as proof of the CDC's pragmatism certain 'progressive' that is, protectionist, policies have been incorporated into the party's political discourse, in addition to measures to protect traditional small businesses from the worst effects of economic deregulation. Such small businesses represent an important source of support for the CiU

The UDC shares much of the political doctrine of the CDC as this is expressed in electoral manifestos and governmental programmes. However, the UDC's ideological position is less pragmatic and more in line with the overall doctrine of Christian democracy and is slightly more conservative than that of the CDC, although, as already noted, differences are minimal given the UDC's reliance on the CDC in electoral terms.

3. Electoral Performance and Profile

The CiU has been by far the most important political force in regional elections, in which it has always won the most seats. After the surprise victory in 1980, although far short of an absolute majority, the CiU went on to obtain absolute majorities in 1984, 1988 and 1992. In 1995 the absolute majority was lost, despite the fact that the actual number of votes rose by more than 100,000, which meant that the CiU was eventually forced to come to an understanding with the PP. The PP allowed the CiU to govern alone in exchange for the CiU's support of the first Aznar government. Although the CiU did not gain the most votes in the elections to the Catalan parliament in 1999, the electoral system gives more weight to representation in rural areas which meant that the CiU, with more seats than its main rival, the PSC, was able to form a government by relying on the parliamentary support of the PP. A similar situation emerged from the recent regional elections of 2003, with two important differences. Firstly the PSC and the CiU saw their overall number of votes, their percentage of total votes cast and the number of seats won decline sharply. Secondly, the CiU was this time unable to achieve a parliamentary alliance with the PP since their combined total of seats was lower than that of the opposition parties of the left, the PSC, the ERC and *Izquierda Unida* (IU). Thus, for the first time since parliamentary democracy was restored to Spain, CiU was forced to hand over the government of the *Generalitat* to the progressive, *catalanista* coalition of the PSC, the ERC and IC-V.

The CiU's rise to power in Catalonia coincided with the collapse of its moderate rival, the UCD, and with an overall shift in the political climate away from the more radical positions held by the ERC. In addition, the PSC was very much constrained in Catalonia by the fact that the PSOE soon became the dominant party in Madrid. Since that time, the CiU, and Pujol in particular, have been very successful in raising their political profile as the defenders of Catalonia in the face of the perceived hostility of successive central governments. Pujol and all of the governments that he presided over maintained high popularity ratings, due in part to the fact that their administration was perceived as being efficiently run.

In terms of voting patterns, the CiU has been helped by two inter-related phenomena: firstly by high levels of abstention among the immigrant population of the industrial belt around Barcelona, whose 'natural' party is the PSC; and, secondly, by the fact that the CiU vote extends beyond 'the traditional areas of support. The CiU is therefore able to capture a significant share of the vote of the salaried, urban population of non-Catalan origin and is able to reach sectors of the centre-right and centre-left',[10] many of whom vote for the PSC in general elections.

In general elections, the reverse has very much been the case, with the CiU consistently relegated to the position of second party, after the PSC–PSOE. Between 1986 and 2000, the CiU attracted approximately 30 per cent of votes cast, although the recent 2004 general elections saw the party lose a substantial share of the vote, dropping to just over 20 per cent. There are two factors which contribute to this relatively poor performance in general elections. Firstly, a number of voters who naturally support the CiU in regional elections, choose to support the PSC-PSOE in general elections. Secondly there are a number of voters who abstain in regional elections but who turn out to vote for the PSC-PSOE in general elections.

The CiU electorate is made up of a slightly higher proportion of women than men and is drawn from older age groups, with the immense majority declaring themselves to be practising Catholics. In terms of place of birth, the majority are from Catalonia, as are their parents. This translates into a sense of national identity which is either 'more Catalan than Spanish' or 'exclusively Catalan', and leads to a prevalence of pro-Catalan nationalist sentiments amongst the electorate in general. On the left-right political spectrum, most CiU voters locate themselves towards the centre. The CiU is seen by its own voters as a pro-Catalan centre party, with the electorate in general expressing a different view by placing it right of centre.[11]

4. The CiU and the Autonomic State

The CiU's overall attitude to the autonomic state and Catalonia's place within it has been characterized, as in many other cases, by ambiguity and pragmatism, although it must be pointed out that CiU supported the 1978 constitution and the 1979 Catalan statute of autonomy, the two documents that currently regulate Catalan self-government within Spain.

The CiU has never presented a clear, definitive plan for the territorial organization of the Spanish state. As late as 1996, Jordi Pujol was still musing over several possible models: confederalism, asymmetric federalism, a mixture of federalism and confederalism, maintaining that no option should be ruled out.[12]

In terms of the specific relation between Catalonia and the Spanish state, the strategy of the CiU, through the *Generalitat*, has been based on ad hoc pragmatism. It has gradually sought to increase the policy powers of the Catalan autonomic institutions at the expense of the state level, without placing a limit on where this may lead, although full independence would appear to have been ruled out, at least for the moment.

These constant demands for more policy-making powers for the *Generalitat* have led to confrontations with various central governments, particularly with the socialist ones of the 1980s that enjoyed an absolute majority. However, this situation of confrontation changed during the 1990s, when the CiU's support was necessary for the formation of both PSOE and PP governments.

Recently, the CiU have put forward various proposals[13] to improve the functioning of the autonomic state, including:

. the reform of the Senate, the upper house, into a chamber of territorial representation, as is the case in federal states such as Germany;
. a 'fairer' finance system, that would allow the *Generalitat* a greater say over how to spend taxes collected in Catalonia;
. the reform of the central state 'peripheral' administration, more mechanisms for cooperation between Autonomous Communities (ACs);
. more AC participation in the EU decision-making process (see below).

At the same time, however, the debate has been opened up within the CiU over the possibility, the necessity, and the desirability of constitutional reform. The main reason for taking such a step would appear to be based on the desire for formal, constitutional recognition of Catalonia's status as a nation, as opposed to the rather fudged current wording that refers to Spain as a 'nation of nationalities' (Catalonia being one of them).

5. The CiU and Europe

Like many other regionalist and nationalist political movements in Europe, the process of European integration is mostly seen as positive by the CiU, since the integration process is perceived as eroding the absolute sovereignty of the member states and thus opens up a whole range of possibilities for the sub-state level of government. In addition, Europe has traditionally represented modernization and openness against the backwardness and inwardness of the Spanish state as it is perceived by Catalan nationalist thought. Thus, the CiU has always been a strong supporter of European integration, on the one hand lending their support to successive governments in Madrid to guarantee political and economic stability to ensure Spain's successful entry into EMU, while on the other, at the institutional level, the *Generalitat* has been at the vanguard of the European regional movement.

The CiU's overall position on Europe and on the question of how Catalonia should articulate its role in Europe, can be divided into two parts. At an abstract level, the CiU continues to support the idea of shared sovereignty between the various levels of government involved, and the idea of a multicultural, multilingual and multinational EU, in which the language and identity of all the nations of the EU, whether they enjoy the condition of statehood or not, should be respected. At a more practical level, in order to take advantage of an increasing number of opportunities for local and regional levels of government to participate in EU policy-making (for example, the EU regional policy), the CiU has consistently sought a series of undertakings from the Spanish state to enable Catalonia and the other ACs to be able to play a more direct role in EU policy-making, especially in those areas that are the policy competence of the ACs and not of the Spanish state, such as agriculture.

Partit dels Socialistes de Catalunya-PSOE (PSC-PSOE)

1. Introduction and Historical Background

The PSC is a sovereign party federated to the PSOE, which reserves its independence to formulate policy on issues which fall within the 'national' ambit of Catalonia, while following the line laid down by the PSOE at federal level on statewide issues.

The current PSC is the result of the merger of various socialist groups in Catalonia in July 1978, with the most important of such groups being the FC-PSOE (Catalan Federation of the PSOE) and the PSC-Congrès (Congress). Since its formation, the PSC has generally been the second electoral force in the regional elections behind the CiU (at least in terms of the number of seats won), while consistently obtaining the most votes in Catalonia in the general elections. The party's strength at the local level, particularly in the city of Barcelona and the principal industrial towns of Catalonia, must also be kept in mind.

The Catalan origins of the two parties which merged to form the PSC, the FC and the PSOE, go back almost one hundred years. These two parties inherited a republican, secular, working-class tradition that looked to the state as a means of establishing socialism. The PSC-C, on the other hand, had its roots in cooperative movements, anarcho-syndicalist and pro-Catalan groups, and thus belongs to a very different socialist tradition to that of the FC-PSOE. These two political cultures still exist to some extent within the PSC today.[14]

During the Franco dictatorship, the various socialist groups were fragmented. On merging in 1978, however, the PSC-PSOE soon replaced the communist *Partit Socialista Unificat de Catalunya* (PSUC) as the leading party of the left in Catalonia. Overall, despite the formal sovereignty that the PSC enjoys, it has encountered difficulties in presenting itself as a truly independent political force. This has meant that in general elections, the PSC has often received the benefits of the PSOE's popularity at the Spanish level, while in regional elections, the reverse has been true, with the PSC losing votes to parties, such as the CiU, that are able to offer a more independent image in the defence of Catalan interests.

2. Party Structure and Membership

Like CDC, the PSC is organized in a pyramidal fashion, consisting of the local level (*agrupaciones*) at the bottom, followed by federations made up of the *agrupaciones*, with the national-level bodies at the top, the most important being the congress, the national council, both legislative bodies, and the national executive commission. Until 2000, the leader of the party, the first secretary, was 'primus inter pares' in what was a collegiate body, while the president of the party was very much an honorary title. This has now changed with Pasqual Maragall taking on the role of party leader from his position as president, while the new first secretary, José Montilla, is responsible for the functioning of the party on a day-to-day basis.

In terms of its organizational structure, power is concentrated at the national level and it is the national executive and the national council that take the key decisions, such as those relating to the drawing up of electoral lists. In this sense 'internal democracy is more apparent than real'.[15] On the other hand, attention must also be drawn to the power of the party apparatus and that of the principal local leaders, commonly referred to as the party 'barons'.[16]

During the period 1978–97, PSC membership grew to reach a figure of 28,000 members, 65 per cent of which are concentrated in the city of Barcelona and the industrial belt that surrounds it, while the majority of the remaining membership is drawn from the *agrupaciones* in the larger industrialized towns in the interior of Catalonia and on the coast. By contrast, the PSC has little presence on the ground in the poorer, rural parts of Catalonia.[17]

In general terms, the PSC membership has traditionally been associated with male, blue-collar industrial workers, the majority of whom are first or second generation immigrants from the rest of Spain, particularly from Andalusia.

3. Ideology

Overall, the ideological line taken by the PSC would appear to be driven by its relations with the PSOE, and thus the PSC's evolution has mirrored that of the PSOE, which has moved from orthodox Marxism to a more moderate, social democratic position, in which the market is accepted as a means of organizing economic activity. On the Catalan national question, the PSC reiterated in the 1996 congress that the party was indeed 'national' and had as its aim the defence 'of a political project for Catalonia, that is, the strengthening of the specific identity of Catalonia and the effective recognition, in all areas, of those national rights that belong to Catalonia'.[18]

In terms of how such a conception of Catalonia is to be formulated, the PSC stops short of claiming the right to national self-determination for Catalonia, and prefers, instead, to talk of federalism and of linking the development of socialism in Catalonia to its development in the rest of the Spanish state.

This federalist vision, that would guarantee the protection of Catalonia's national rights, forms part of a long tradition within the Spanish left, which goes back over one hundred years. A key element of the PSC's federalist project is the concept of subsidiarity, the idea that political decisions must be taken at the closest level possible to the citizen, a concept which relates closely to the municipal socialist tradition within the PSC.

4. Electoral Performance and Profile

In the regional elections, the PSC soon became the unquestioned leader of the left in Catalonia and the main opposition party to the CiU in the Catalan parliament, after the initial disappointment of the first election results in 1980. The share of votes obtained by the PSC has consistently remained at around the 30 per cent level until 1995 when the figure dropped to 24 per cent. This was due, to some extent, to internal differences within the party and also to the problems experienced by the PSOE in general. However, the 1999 regional elections saw a major change of fortune for the PSC, as the charismatic former mayor of Barcelona, Pasqual Maragall, in coalition with the civic platform *Ciutadans pel Canvi* (Citizens for Change (CpC)) and with *IC-Verds* in the provinces outside Barcelona, succeeded in winning more votes than the ruling nationalist coalition, the CiU. However, due to the electoral system in Catalonia, and in Spain in general, in which fewer votes from rural areas are required to elect parliamentary deputies, the CiU succeeded in winning one more seat (to take their total to fifty-six) than Maragall's combined forces, given the concentration of the latter's vote in urban areas. This situation has been repeated in the recent regional elections of November 2003, although both the PSC and the CiU have experienced a decline as other parties have gained a greater share of the vote. Despite this decline, however, the president of the PSC, Pasquall Maragall has been sworn in as the new president of the government of the *Generalitat*, with the support of both the ERC and IC-V.

In the general elections, the PSC has been a source of support for the PSOE, with the PSC always coming first in Catalonia and regularly obtaining 40 per cent of the vote. Indeed, in the general elections of 1996, in which the PSOE lost power in Madrid to the PP, the PSC saw its percentage share of the vote increase, contrary to the general trend of decline elsewhere in Spain. While not suffering the debacle of the PSOE in general in the general elections of 2000, the PSC nevertheless experienced a decline in both the number and the percentage of the vote gained, which prompted the resignation of the first secretary, Narcís Serra and paved the way for Pasqual Maragall to take over the leadership of the party. This change in party leadership has coincided with a reversal in the electoral fortunes of the PSC, and in the 2004 general elections the party obtained a 40 per cent share of votes cast in Catalonia, returning the party to its previous levels of electoral popularity.

In order to explain the striking difference between the results of the PSC in the general and regional elections, reference must be made to the phenomenon of the dual vote in Catalonia. Until 1999, the PSC had failed to capture much of the middle-class urban 'Catalan' vote in the regional elections, due mainly to the perception that the PSC was not the best party to defend Catalonia's desire for self-government against the seemingly centralist PSOE governments in Madrid. The prospects for regional electoral success have also suffered, as noted above, due to high levels of abstention amongst 'natural' socialist voters, particularly those from other parts of Spain, who show little interest in Catalan politics. In the 1999 elections, Maragall was able to overcome the reticence of many middle-class voters, particularly those in Barcelona, who tend to vote for the CiU in regional elections. This was due, above all, to his image as a politician dedicated to the Catalan cause, acting independently of the PSOE in Madrid, and was also due to his success as mayor of Barcelona.

There is an almost even split amongst PSC voters between women and men. PSC voters also tend to be middle-aged and working class and to be less well-educated than the supporters of the other parties. The majority of PSC voters were either born outside Catalonia, or have parents who were. This is reflected in the choice of language with Castilian being the language most used in the home, among friends and in the workplace. However, in terms of national identity, most feel 'equally Spanish and Catalan', although up to 20 per cent said that they felt 'only Spanish'. The vast majority of voters when asked to position themselves on the left-right ideological scale, declare themselves to be either on the left or centre-left.[19]

5. The PSC and the Autonomic State

Until recently, the PSC has had problems in expressing its vision of the autonomic state due to the fact that it is generally perceived by voters to be dependent on the PSOE. In some cases this perception is born out by fact, although the opposition party status of the PSOE between 1996 and 2004 allowed for more independence for the PSC on this issue. On the return of the PSOE to power in Madrid in 2004, the new prime minister, José Luis Rodríguez Zapatero reiterated his electoral promise to respect the new statute of Catalan autonomy which was approved by the Catalan parliament in 2005. However, the Socialist leader must tread a fine line between satisfying the demands of all Catalan parties for more self-government – including the PSC – and appeasing those of a more centralist tendency within the PSOE. For its part, the PSC has moved beyond its traditional formulation of general proposals for a federal Spain and has put forward a number of more concrete proposals for the development of the autonomic state. Certain of these proposals bear a resemblance to the plans put forward by the CiU. Three main areas can be highlighted:[20]

- An increase in self-government for the ACs and further de-centralization of the Spanish state, including a clearer definition of policy competences between the ACs, the central government and local authorities, and the reduction of the 'peripheral' administration of the state in the ACs;
- An increase in mechanisms for cooperation between the ACs and for their participation at the state level, with special emphasis on the reform of the Senate, with the aim of converting it into a house of genuine territorial representation along federal lines;
- A more transparent system of finance for the ACs, which must incorporate elements of inter-AC solidarity to ensure socio-economic cohesion between all the ACs of the Spanish state, whilst at the same time including a greater proportion of taxes

collected in each AC earmarked for the financing of the AC in question.

6. The PSC and Europe

The PSC's position on Europe is very clear: 'The construction of Europe is seen by Catalonia as being positive for all Europeans and especially so for the Catalans . . . we are convinced that the European dimension can provide the framework for the development of our collective expectations. We must be conscious of the fact that our future is Europe'.[21] Catalonia, in this sense, 'must be able to integrate itself into a multinational state and not into a multi-state nation'.[22] In other words, the PSC supports the emergence of some form of European state, but this state must respect the cultural and linguistic traditions of all the nations that make up the EU, and not just the nation states that currently exist. Thus, the PSC proposes two main types of relationship between Catalonia and the EU. Firstly, it proposes that Catalonia should be linked to Europe via the Spanish state. Secondly, Catalonia should establish a direct relationship with Europe via the institutionalization of the European regional movement and, in particular, through the Committee of the Regions, set up by the Maastricht Treaty in 1994, The Committee of the Regions, however, has yet to fulfil the expectations that it raised at the outset.

As in the case of the PSC doctrine on the relationship between Catalonia and the Spanish state, federalism and subsidiarity are seen as the best way of structuring the relationship between Catalonia and Europe, given that 'federalism is more efficient, respectful and is more democratic',[23] representing a guarantee that Europe will respect the pluralism of its cultural and political diversity.

Esquerra Republicana de Catalunya (ERC)

1. Introduction and Historical Background

The ERC is an historic, left-wing, republican, nationalist political formation that openly calls for independence for Catalonia. While the CiU could be considered the most important political force in Catalonia since the restoration of democracy, without doubt it is the ERC that lays claim to being the most important party in historical terms. During the eight years of the Second Republic (1931–9), the ERC presided over the regional government, the *Generalitat de Catalunya*, which enjoyed almost unprecedented levels of political autonomy. Even with the fall of Catalonia and the execution of the president of the *Generalitat*, Lluís Companys, the ERC kept the flame alive by maintaining the institutions of the regional government in exile. However, since the end of Franco's dictatorship, the ERC has been unable to recover its hegemonic position.

The ERC was founded in 1931 as the meeting point of various left-wing and nationalist political groupings, ranging from the pro-independence *Estat Català* (Catalan State) to Lluís Company's *Partit Republicà Català* (Catalan Republican Party) and other, less organized groups in favour of independence, federal republicanism or trade unionism.

Perhaps the key defining feature of the ERC is its insistence on political recognition of the Catalan nation, with full sovereignty being the ultimate goal. The party's republicanism meant that it was not legalized until after the first democratic general elections of 1977 and, consequently, the party opposed the constitution in the referendum of 1978. Despite such opposition, and its pro-independence ideology, the ERC has since participated fully in political life at all levels, even sending deputies to the Madrid parliament.

After the ERC had lost some of its support due to the perception that the party had become excessively moderate, the late 1980s saw the beginning of a process of reaffirmation of the pro-independence position of the ERC. This was followed by an increased emphasis on more radically left-wing socio-economic concerns. Currently, the party has just obtained the best general election results of its recent history, and, although it still remained far from its hegemonic position of the 1930s, recent regional election results have seen the ERC return to a coalition government in Catalonia for the first time since the early 1980s.

2. Party Structure and Membership

The ERC, like most of the other parties studied in this chapter, is organized along territorial lines, with the base formed by the local level, followed by the county, regional and, finally, the national level, which forms the peak of the pyramidal structure. Once more, the national level is dominated by three main institutions: the congress, which meets every three years and is the supreme legislative body, the national council, which decides on policies governing the (regional) congresses, including those relating to the control of the executive and to the approval of the general lines of election manifestos, and finally, the executive committee, 'the main governing body of the party, which is made up of a wide-ranging membership including representatives from the national council, regional presidents, leaders of the youth section, the *Joves Esquerra Republicana de Catalunya* (JERC), and the ERC spokespersons in the various parliaments'.[24] In general, the internal party structure is not as hierarchical as that of some of the other parties in this chapter. All members, for example, have the right to attend the congress. The executive committee, too, would appear to be highly representative of all sections of the party, although perhaps as a result of this breadth, there exists within the executive committee a permanent political commission, 'a restricted organ that holds the real power within the ERC'.[25]

According to the party, membership has greatly increased over the last decade, with the number of members going from approximately 6,000 in 1990 to almost 10,000 by the end of the 1990s. In terms of the sociological profile of party members, a survey of delegates to the nineteenth national congress in 1993 concluded[26] that the core members of the ERC are predominantly young, male and middle class, and live in large or small towns, with the majority having been born in Catalonia, of Catalan-born parents, and with an overwhelming majority using the Catalan language almost exclusively. The same members located themselves and the party to the left of the political spectrum and were willing to adopt the most radical positions on the question of Catalan independence.

3. Ideology

Since its legalization in 1978, the ERC has 'undergone an erratic ideological evolution',[27] as it found difficulty, particularly in the late 1970s and 1980s, in adapting to the new political environment. From the radical left-wing, pro-independence positions of the 1970s, the party drifted towards a more moderate ideological line, reflected in its willingness to enter into two governmental coalitions with the CiU in the *Generalitat* (1980–7). To counteract such a trend, from the mid 1980s onwards there was a progressive incorporation into the party of pro-independence groupings, which even included more moderate sections of the armed separatist group, *Terra Lluire* (Free Homeland). This transition was completed with the naming of Àngel Colom as the new party leader, and set the scene for a new, more radical ideological orientation of the party, particularly with regard to the question of independence for Catalonia. The new party statutes of 1992 and the ideological declaration of 1993 are the foundation for the current ideological line of the party. The new statutes declare the ERC to be 'a political party founded in 1931 that seeks the territorial unity and the independence of the Catalan nation through the construction of its own state within the framework of Europe'.[28] The Catalan nation is defined mainly in historical, cultural, linguistic and territorial terms and, in the latter sense, includes all of the *Països Catalans* of Valencia, the Balearic Islands and Roussillon in southern France, all of which are historic Catalan territories where the Catalan language is still spoken. The Catalan people, as a nation, naturally enjoy national rights such as the preservation of their culture, language, traditions and so forth, and in the ERC's opinion the best way of guaranteeing such rights is within the framework of the nation state.

While the goal of independence was reaffirmed in the early 1990s and was subsequently maintained, the new leadership of the ERC, headed by Josep-Lluís Carod-Rovira has tried to develop the party's doctrine on socio-economic issues. The party would seem to offer moderate, social-democratic solutions given its 'will to defend the welfare state and the intervention of the state in the market in order to eliminate social and territorial inequalities'.[29]

4. Electoral Performance and Profile

After the relative success in the regional elections of 1980, the party suffered a series of electoral setbacks in all types of elections, due to a party leadership crisis and due to its transformation, in the eyes of many voters, into a mere satellite party of the CiU. The restructuring of the party and the new pro-independence line adopted from 1992 onwards bore fruits, after 'bottoming out' in the 1988 regional elections and the 1989 general elections. In addition to better overall results in the 1990s, the ERC also witnessed the effects of the dual vote, obtaining better results in the regional than in the general elections, due mainly to the transfer of support for the PSC to the ERC in the regional elections.[30] The 1999 elections were considered to be an essential test for the ERC, given the perceived bi-polarization of the electoral contest and the fact that the erstwhile party leader, Àngel Colom, had abandoned the ERC to form his own party, the Independence Party (PI) threatening to split the ERC vote. Despite such difficult circumstances, the ERC's share of the vote was just one percentage point less than the result in 1995, which had been considered a good one. While the general elections of March 2000 confirmed the ERC's full reinstatement as an important, if not decisive, electoral force in Catalonia, then the regional elections of November 2003 show a doubling of support for the party when compared to the results of the 1999 elections. The ERC doubled its total number of votes (from just over 250,000 to over 500,000), doubled its percentage of total vote (from 8.65 per cent to 16.4 per cent), and doubled its number of seats (from twelve to twenty-three), effectively giving the party the decisive say in the composition of the new government of the Generalitat.

The results of the 2004 general election confirmed the rise of the ERC, with the party increasing its number of votes from just over 190,000 in 2000 to almost 638,000. At the same time, the ERC went from holding just one seat in the Madrid parliament to eight, turning the ERC into a power broker, in that the minority socialist government of Rodríguez Zapatero depends on the ERC for its parliamentary majority.

In general, the ERC electorate shares many of the features of CiU voters in terms of their geographical distribution. Voters tend to be drawn from the rural areas away from the industrial belt of Barcelona. In many cases, especially in rural Lleida and Girona, the ERC is the second party behind the CiU.[31]

Over the last two decades, ERC voter profiles have changed from members of the older generation voters, who still identified with the ERC of the Second Republic, to a younger, more progressive electorate. In addition ERC voters are mainly male, were born in Catalonia, of Catalan parents, and show the highest levels of use of the Catalan language in all areas of daily life. Thus, it is no surprise to learn that the vast majority of ERC voters consider themselves to be either more Catalan than Spanish or exclusively Catalan. On the left-right scale of political values, ERC voters tend to position themselves and the party at the left of the scale, further to the left, even, than the *Iniciativa per Catalunya* (IC), while core voters are more moderate, situating themselves more towards the centre.[32]

5. The ERC and the Autonomic State

Two things must be noted before proceeding with any analysis of the ERC's position with regard to the autonomic state. In the first place, the ERC voted in favour of the Catalan statute of autonomy, since 'the only alternative to scarcely any political autonomy offered in the Statute was absolutely none'.[33] Secondly, the ERC is the only political party in Catalonia that openly defends independence as the best political option for Catalonia. Thus it could be concluded that, in general terms, the ERC was very much against the autonomic state. However, since becoming party leader, Carod-Rovira has tried to develop a more pragmatic line on Catalonia's role within the Spanish state. While independence remains the overall goal, the ERC has developed a series of political proposals on the reform of the autonomic state, which reflect the need for pragmatism on the part of the ERC, although they still go beyond the demands of the other parties.[34] These include:

- Demands for the completion of the transfer of policy powers already foreseen in the existing statute of autonomy and the constitution;
- A new 'national' statute that establishes bilateral relations between Spain and Catalonia, introducing the concept of equality between the two nations;
- In terms of finance, the party seeks the establishment of the confederal finance system enjoyed by the Basque provinces and Navarre, whereby all the taxes collected in the community in question remain there, and negotiation then takes place with the state as to how much is to be paid, if anything, for central government services;
- The political articulation of the *Països Catalans*, including the possibility of a federation between the current ACs that collectively form the *Països Catalans*, something explicitly forbidden by the current Constitution;
- The reform of the Senate, not along federal lines, whereby all ACs enjoy the same status, but instead along the lines of a new Senate in which the different nationalities of Spain are represented.

6. The ERC and Europe

The ERC strongly supports the EU for two basic reasons. On the one hand, as noted above, Europe has always been an important element of Catalanism, while on the other, the ERC recognizes the inevitability of European integration in political, economic and social terms, and thus, for Catalonia it is of vital importance not to 'miss the boat'.

In terms of party strategy, the ERC is basically pragmatic, recognizing the major role that the nation states have played up until now in the integration process, and the role that they will continue to play. Within this framework, the ERC calls for the establishment of a European federation, with a real European government fully accountable to the European Parliament. Within such a federation, however, the ERC perceives an inevitable process of political decentralization to the level of the regions and, importantly, the existence of many nations without states, such as Catalonia. These must have direct access to the EU institutions, particularly in areas where they already enjoy exclusive policy competences. At the same time, while promoting regionalism in general, the ERC stresses that Catalonia, as a nation, must be treated differently from 'mere' regions, and in this respect, in addition to more direct access to the European institutions, the ERC seeks to establish Catalonia as a separate electoral constituency for European elections, instead of being 'diluted' in a single Spanish one, as is currently the case.

Iniciativa per Catalunya-Els Verds (IC-V)

1. Introduction and Historical Background

The IC-V is a post-communist, environmentalist political formation that was born out of the crisis of the left and of the emergence of a new political agenda that included environmentalism, feminism, pacifism, and concerns over the developing world. The IC came to life as a result of the coming together of several communist political formations in Catalonia, among which the PSUC was the most important. After three years of electoral coalition with various environmentalist groups, the IC finally took the decision to rename itself IC-V in 1998, formalizing the acceptance of green issues as one of the key ideological reference points for the party.

The history of the IC-V is, above all, the history of the PSUC, the most important Marxist-inspired political party of the Second Republic and a leading political force in the defence of Catalonia in the Civil War, which formed part of the overall communist offensive to control the anti-Fascist struggle.[35] During the long years of Franco's dictatorship, the PSUC emerged as the main clandestine political opposition group to the dictatorship to the point where not only sectors of the working class were active in the party, but where an increasingly number of left-wing intellectuals also became involved. The internal ideological crisis within the party, and the increasing popularity of the Socialist Party, led to the collapse of the PSUC as a serious electoral force in the early 1980s. However, by the mid 1980s, hope emerged for the PSUC as the Socialist Party moved to the right and, pacifist and left-wing groups had successfully campaigned in Catalonia against Spain remaining in NATO, all of which demonstrated that political space continued to exist on the left in Catalonia. Thus, in 1987 three communist formations came together to form the IC, at first as a federation of parties, and subsequently as a sovereign party in its own right.

Since its foundation, two processes can be highlighted:

. In organizational terms, the IC has striven to consolidate itself as a sovereign party, creating its own new organizational structure to substitute that of the founding members. This led to the *Partit dels Comunistes de Catalunya* (PCC), one of the founding parties, breaking away;
. In ideological terms, there has been a clear distancing from communism, and a move towards a more flexible political doctrine that has taken on board many issues of the 'New Left', which led to the IC breaking ties with Izquierda Unida, and the latter encouraging the setting up of the *Esquerra Unida i Alternativa* (EUiA – United and Alternative Left) in Catalonia, to rival the IC-V.

All of these attempts to consolidate the party have come up against a general crisis of the left, which in Catalonia has led to a general fragmentation of the left-wing political forces, and the consequent weakening of the IC-V as a political force.

2. Party Structure and Membership

After the first three years of life when the IC operated as a federation of the three founding parties, the 1st national assembly in 1990 paved the way for the federation to take on an increasing number of responsibilities, with the overall aim being the total absorption of the founding parties, and the formation of a unified party with its own structure. However, from the beginning, the IC wanted to avoid the problems that it felt other parties were experiencing, such as excessive hierarchy, too few mechanisms for the participation of members and too little contact with non-party groups. Thus, the IC sought to ensure plural, meaningful and ongoing debates within the party, and sought to create more openness to guarantee the participation of groups from the rest of society, such as student associations, trades unions and NGOs. However, despite the will to introduce new forms of party political activity, the current organizational structure differs little from that of the other parties analysed in the current chapter. It consists of a base level, made up of territorial, sectoral, and issue-orientated groups, with the addition, in this case, of groups in the work place. Above the base level is the intermediate level that groups together several of the base-level groupings, with the national level at the top, which includes the major legislative and executive bodies of the party. Thus it is unclear whether its original objectives have been achieved, since 'the process of political renewal was carried out without modifying the internal organization and without producing a real change in the party cadres'.[36]

In 1996, the IC had almost 8,000 members, over 80 per cent of whom were concentrated in the city of Barcelona and in the industrial towns that surround it. With the opening up of the party to environmental groups, the party has attracted younger, middle-class members, often employed in public sector administration, although the party remains dominated by men, with over 74 per cent of the membership being male.

3. Ideology

The IC-V, like the vast majority of communist parties, has witnessed changes in its political doctrine over the last twenty years. This journey in search of new ideological reference points has involved abandoning orthodox Marxism, as a doctrine that sought to provide answers to all the challenges facing society, and the embracing of a more plural, flexible political agenda that seeks to provide answers to specific problems. In this context, the party now defines itself as the 'eco-socialist left',[37] which seeks ways to transform society based on the values of social justice, solidarity, gender difference, equality of opportunities, freedom, peace, national rights, emancipation and environmental sustainability. Rather than present each of these values separately, the IC-V seeks to include them within an overall ideological framework, whose Marxist roots are still partly in evidence. Thus their proposal to change society 'is based on the analysis of the diverse contradictions that preside over capitalism, contradictions derived from the exploitation of labour and the unjust distribution and appropriation of its fruits, both between social classes and economic regions and peoples'.[38]

On the question of Catalan nationalism, the IC-V ideology could be considered to consist of a combination of the nationalism of the ERC and the federalism of the PSC, which at times has proved a difficult balancing act to perform. On the one hand, Catalonia is perceived as a nation, based on a cultural identity which gives rise to a political will that seeks political recognition of the Catalan nation. As such, 'IC-V affirms that the sovereignty of Catalonia resides in the people, which has the full right to seek self-determination'[39] in order to ensure the defence and protection of its full development as a national community. However, the IC-V stops short of demanding outright independence for Catalonia and, instead, given that all peoples have the right to self-determination, is of the opinion that the best way of guaranteeing solidarity among distinct communities is federalism. Thus, in the Spanish context the IC-V calls for a federal state, based on national self-determination and the full political recognition of the multi-national personality of the state.

4. Electoral Performance and Profile

Unfortunately for the party, the best results obtained by the IC-V, were those of its principal founder, the PSUC, at the beginning of the post-Franco era, when they obtained 17 per cent of the votes cast in the general elections of 1979 and 18 per cent in the regional elections of the following year. The internal crisis within the party led to a dramatic decline in the PSUC vote, with the party gaining just 4.5 per cent of the vote in the general elections of 1982, with the 'deserters'

either choosing to abstain or voting for the PSC, which quickly consolidated itself as the leading party of the left in Catalonia.

After the internal renovation of the party and the subsequent
setting up of the IC, the results began to improve, a process mirrored
in the rest of Spain by the *Partido Comunista de España-Izquierda
Unida* (PCE-IU). By the regional elections of 1995, the party's share
of the vote had reached almost 10 per cent, to the general satisfaction
of the IC-V coalition. The regional elections of 1999 represented a
new political scenario for the IC-V, as the party leadership took the
brave decision to form an electoral coalition with the *Partit dels
Socialistes de Catalunya-Ciutadans pel Canvi* (PSC-CpC) in the three
provinces outside that of Barcelona, while in the province of
Barcelona, the IC-V presented its own electoral lists. In the latter
province, the IC-V obtained just 3.3 per cent of the vote, a poor result
when compared with the figure of 12.5 per cent in 1995. In many
cases this loss was due to the fact that many voters chose to vote
directly for Maragall's coalition, while another share of the vote, 14
per cent, went to the rival, breakaway group the EUiA.[40] This trend
continued during the elections of March 2000, with the IC-V losing
almost a third of the votes it obtained in 1996, with many going to
EUiA and with many of the remainder of voters abstaining.
However, the IC-V, like the ERC and the PP, benefited both from the
decline of both the PSC and the CiU in the regional elections of
2003, and from the fact that it presented joint lists with the breakaway
group, the EUiA, in all Catalan electoral districts. The results were
most significant, with the party receiving 240,000 votes in total,
compared with just 78,000 four years previously, while in terms of the
number of seats, the IC-V obtained a total of twelve, nine more than
in 1999, all of which has allowed the IC-V to enter into the new
government of Pasqual Maragall.

In terms of the party's performance in general elections, given that
IC-V has represented the state-wide PCE-IU at all general elections
since 1977, the former's electoral fortunes have very much mirrored
the latter's. From the heights of the late 1970s when the IC-V fore-
runner, the PSUC, obtained approximately 18 per cent of votes,
almost two decades later the party's support in general elections was
maintained at around 7 per cent of the electorate. The split with
EUiA, which meant that in the 2000 elections EUiA represented IU
in the general elections in Catalonia, saw the IC-V's votes drop to just
over 2 per cent, a figure that would rise to almost 6 per cent in the

subsequent 2004 general election, when both parties presented joint lists.

In geographic terms, the electoral profile of the IC-V mirrors that of the PSC. The majority of the IC-V vote is concentrated in the same areas as the PSC vote, that is urban, industrial areas, in and around the city of Barcelona. In recent years the sociological profile of IC-V voters has undergone a transformation from the traditional working-class, unionized, middle-aged male voter of the PSUC, to a younger electorate, employed in the service sector, with relatively high levels of education and interest in politics. IC-V voters continue to define themselves as left-wing, but this identification is now more moderate than in the 1980s. The IC-V holds a wide spectrum of positions on the question of Catalan self-government, ranging from pro-independence to much more moderate positions.[41]

5. The IC-V and the Autonomic State

'The principal problem for the IC-V is in differentiating itself from other political forces on the question of the development of self-government'.[42] In this sense, the principal problem comes with the overlap with the proposals put forward by the PSC for a federal model and, thus, the IC-V prefers to talk instead of asymmetric federalism, which in fact takes it closer to the CiU. This is further reinforced by the IC-V's insistence on the right for national self-determination. Beyond these doctrinal considerations, the IC-V put forward specific proposals for the improvement of the present model, not just for Catalonia but for the autonomic state as a whole, and which include:

- The simplification and decentralization of the 'peripheral' administration of the central state to allow a clearer role for the autonomic political institutions and a bigger role for the local authorities;
- The completion of the process of transfer of policy competences foreseen in the respective statutes of autonomy;
- The introduction of a new finance system that guarantees transparency, accountability and solidarity, whereby each AC would collect taxes in their territorial ambit and then pay a certain amount to the state, such amount to be decided by a reformed Senate;

- The reformed Senate would be a chamber of representatives of the nations and regions of Spain in which the former would enjoy certain privileges. This reform would be part of an overall constitutional reform that would convert Spain into a fully federal state with an element of asymmetry to guarantee the rights of the nations that make up the Spanish state.

6. The IC-V and Europe

The IC-V strongly supports the idea of a federal, decentralized Europe, in order to defend the 'social and environmental quality of life' for European citizens, a position which mirrors its views on the development of the autonomic state. At the institutional level, the IC-V stresses the need to democratize the European institutions and to introduce an elected European government. In addition the IC-V emphasizes the need to ensure the full application of the principle of subsidiarity, whereby political decisions are taken at the closest possible level to the citizen. In terms of socio-economic reforms, while recognizing the importance of economic and monetary union for macro-economic stability, the IC-V insist that the EU must strengthen economic and social cohesion, not merely as a principle that accompanies the establishment of a European free market, but as a basic principle that informs all EU socio-economic policy making.

El Partit Popular (PP)

1. Introduction and Historical Background

Of all the political parties in Catalonia, the PP has found it most difficult to adapt to the political system in Catalonia, due mainly to its lack of independence from the statewide party, but due also to the fact that the PP itself has been associated with centralizing tendencies, generally perceived to be at odds with self-government in Catalonia. Thus, even at the height of the PP's popularity in Spain as a whole, the PP never went beyond being the third party in Catalonia, enjoying much lower levels of electoral support than those achieved in Spain as a whole.

The founding of the *Alianza Popular* (AP), later to become the PP, in Catalonia, mirrored its development in the rest of Spain, in that the figures closely connected to the defunct Franco regime were behind the setting up of the AP in Catalonia. The electorate identified the AP with the continuation of Francoism, and the elitist structure of the party which lacked a presence on the ground and lacked party activists led to poor election results.[43] In the first regional elections of 1980, where the AP presented itself under the name of *Solidaritat Catalana* (Catalan Solidarity), the party obtained just 2 per cent of the vote. Over time the electoral results have gradually improved, with certain fluctuations remaining and with a clear divergence between the results in the general and regional elections.

The ideological line taken by the PP in Catalonia clearly reflects its subordination to the central party in Madrid, and thus differs very little from the latter's ideological position. This subordination is also reflected in the changes in the regional leadership of the party, which have frequently been driven by the central party according to its needs at the state level. Thus, in 1993, when the PP in Madrid wished to attack the PSOE government and its parliamentary partner, the CiU, José María Aznar imposed the figure of Aleix Vidal-Quadras, anti-Catalan nationalist *par excellence*, who in turn was sacrificed when the PP was obliged to reach a similar agreement with the CiU in 1996. Thus Vidal-Quadras was substituted by the more moderate figure of Alberto Fernández Díaz, who in turn gave way to Josep Piqué, a member of two Aznar governments in Madrid, to head the party's candidature in the 2003 regional elections.

2. Ideology

The ideological line taken by the Catalan PP corresponds to that of the PP at state level and thus little can be added here. However, the Catalan PP has attempted to develop its doctrine on the national question in Catalonia, particularly over the last four years when the PP in Catalonia has tried to establish itself more firmly in Catalonia. However, this does not mean that the party in Catalonia has embraced nationalism. Instead, the current position taken by the party recognizes the cultural, historic and linguistic factors that differentiate Catalonia from other communities in Spain, but nevertheless regards such differences in the context of the overall framework of the Spanish nation state. The aim of the PP in Catalonia is to seek ways to integrate Catalonia into Spain, while preserving the former's defining characteristics.

3. Electoral Performance and Profile

In overall terms, the electoral results of the PP have improved significantly from the very modest beginnings of the general elections in 1979
and the regional elections of 1980, when it obtained just 3.6 per cent
and 2.4 per cent of the overall vote respectively. After the collapse of the
moderate reformist party, the *Unión de Centro Democrático* (UCD),
headed by Adolfo Suárez, the AP saw its results improve dramatically
in Catalonia, reaching 14.6 per cent and achieving parliamentary
representation in all of the Catalan provinces in 1982. However, the effect
did not last, and many of the former UCD voters turned to the CiU
and even to the PSC, with the PP vote stagnating at around 10 per
cent in the general elections, and dropping to even lower levels in the
regional elections. The PP in Catalonia benefited from the wholesale
changes in the PP at state level associated with the rise to power of José
María Aznar, obtaining almost 17 per cent of the vote in the general
elections of 1993, and an equally spectacular 13 per cent in the regional
elections in 1995. After gaining a lower than expected increase in the
1996 general elections, the PP made a notable advance in 2000, to gain
almost 23 per cent of the vote, and appeared to have established itself
as the third party, in general elections at least. However, the general
elections of 2004, in line with trends at state level, saw a drop in the PP's
support in Catalonia, whereby the party gained just over 15 per cent
of votes cast, while in terms of seats gained the party lost half of the
twelve seats won in 2000. In the regional elections of 1999, the PP
actually lost ground, seeing its percentage of votes cast reduced to 9.5
per cent, although evidence exists that many of these voters, given the
split in the vote between Maragall's coalition, PSC-CpC-IC-V, and
Pujol's CiU, chose to vote for the latter as a means of avoiding a
socialist victory. In the regional elections of 2003, the PP substantially
improved its results compared with four years previously, with the
party gaining 12 per cent of total votes cast and fifteen seats in the
Catalan parliament. However, to some extent this was a pyrrhic victory,
in that the decline of the CiU meant that the two parties were unable
to obtain sufficient parliamentary support to continue in government.

   Thus, in addition to the overall progression of the PP vote in Catalonia,
account must be taken, once more, of the 'dual vote' effect, in this case
favouring the PP at general elections, whilst putting them at a disadvantage in the regional elections, with voters either abstaining or
voting for the CiU in the latter.

In terms of the geographical distribution of the PP vote, the party has moved on from a position of relative strength outside the province of Barcelona, where it inherited part of the now defunct UCD electorate, to enjoying increasing popularity in urban areas such as the city of Barcelona and its metropolitan area. The sociological profile of the PP electorate has also changed compared to its profile at the beginning of the democratic period, when it was characterized by relatively old, well-off rentiers, born outside Catalonia, with Catholic right-wing *españolista* political beliefs.[44] The more moderate, liberal image projected by the party since the second half of the 1990s has managed to attract younger, urban voters, especially from non-Catalan backgrounds.

Despite this new moderate image, the PP is still perceived by the electorate at large to be the most right-wing of the political parties in Catalonia, and the most pro-Spanish, an attitude which is felt to undermine Catalonia's ambitions for self-government.

Overall Conclusions

At the beginning of the new democratic era in Catalan politics, the PSC emerged from the shadow of the communist PSUC as the principal party of the left, with the CiU replacing the ERC as the leading political force of Catalan nationalism. Subsequent elections revealed a pattern of an 'alternating' two-party system, whereby the PSC-PSOE has consistently gained the most votes at general and local elections, while the CiU won six consecutive regional elections to the *Parlament de Catalunya.*

However, in recent years the duopoly of both the PSC and CiU has come under increasing threat, and in recent regional and general elections, the sum of both parties' votes has hardly surpassed 60 per cent of the electorate. The relative stability of the party system, dominated as it has been by PSC and CiU, appears to have given rise to a more fluid, less stable situation which raises a series of questions about how the parties will seek accommodation within the emerging party system.

In this new scenario, the PP in Catalonia appears to have taken advantage of the rise in popularity of the party at state level to become a key actor in the political system. However, if recent tendencies continue, it is ERC that has emerged as a decisive force not just in Catalan politics but also in Spanish politics. If in 2003 ERC was wooed by both the PSC and CiU to lend its support to possible government coalitions, the results of the 2004 general elections have meant that the minority socialist government of José Luis Rodríguez Zapatero depends on ERC's parliamentary support, giving the party a degree of power that seemed unlikely only a few years ago. The downside, for the moment at least, is represented by the nationalist federation of parties, the CiU. Internally, Jordi Pujol's successful and charismatic leadership of the CiU federation gave it a degree of internal political stability which allowed it to claim its place at the fulcrum of the political system in Catalonia. Pujol's semi-retirement has created a vacuum that has only partially been filled by the new CiU leader and secretary general of CDC, Artur Mas. Continued electoral failure could well prompt a leadership challenge from within the federation, with UDC leader and rival of Mas for the leadership of the federation Josep Antoni Duran i Lleida an obvious candidate. Such internal tensions may be reinforced by external factors, related to the increasing electoral success of the ERC and the PP. On the one hand, ERC has already begun to attract the more nationalist sectors of CiU voters and members, while on the other there exists the risk of losing to the PP from the right of the federation, particularly but not exclusively from the UDC. Thus, the CiU must walk a fine line if it is to maintain a differentiated political identity.

In terms of the party system itself, it is difficult to predict future scenarios on the basis of recent election results, the decline of the two main parties, the CiU and the PSC in favour of the other three parties, the ERC, the IC-V and the PP, seeming to point in the direction of an end to the dual party system in favour of a more multiparty one in which absolute parliamentary majorities are a thing of the past. However, whatever the outcome of post-Pujolism, what is clear is that a certain process of realignment has begun in political life in Catalonia, and, as in the 1980s, it may be some time before we can talk of a relatively stable party system.

Figure 3.0: Election Results 1979–2004 (percentage of votes cast)

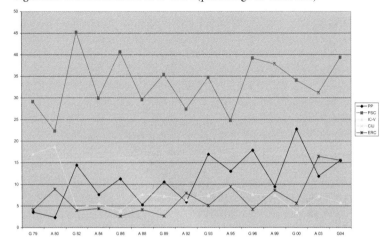

Note: In 1999 autonomic elections IC-V presented its own electoral list in the province of Barcelona, joining the PSC-Ciutadans pel Canvi coalition in the remaining three provinces. In 2004, IC-V formed an electoral coalition with EuiA.

Source: Llebaria Soler, Josep, "Las elecciones autonómicas en Cataluña (1980–1995)", in Manuel de Alcántara and Antonia Martínez (eds), *Las elecciones autonómicas en España (1980–1997)*, Madrid, CIS, 1998.

Suggested Further Reading

Two texts that give a useful overview of the history and development of Catalan nationalism are:

Guibernau, M. (2004) *Catalan Nationalism*. London: Routledge/ Canada Blanch Studies on Contemporary Spain.
McRoberts, K. (2001) *Catalonia: Nation Building Without a State*. Oxford: Oxford University Press.

Notes

[1] M. Baras and J. Matas, 'Els partits polítics i el sistema de partits', in M. Caminal and J. Matas (eds), *El Sistema Polític de Catalunya* (Barcelona: Tecnos, 1998) p.162.

[2] J. Marcet, 'The parties of non-state ambit: the case of Catalonia', in L. de Winter (ed), *Non-State Wide Parties in Europe* (Barcelona: ICPS, 1995), p.71.

[3] Antonio Santamaría, *Foro Babel: El Nacionalismo y las Lenguas de Cataluña* (Barcelona: Ediciones Áltera, 1999).

[4] Isidre Molas (ed), *Diccionari dels Partits Polítics de Catalunya* (Barcelona: Enciclopèdia Catalana, Barcelona, 2000) p. 322.

[5] J. Marcet and J. Argelaguet, 'Nationalist parties in Catalonia', in L. de Winter and H. Türsan (eds), *Regionalist Parties in Western Europe* (London: Routledge, 1998), p. 78.

[6] J. Soler Llebaria, 'Las elecciones autonómicas en Cataluña (1980–1995)', in M. Alcántara and A. Martínez (eds), *Las Elecciones Autonómicas en España, 1980–1997* (Madrid: CIS, 1998) p. 232.

[7] Molas, *Diccionari dels Partits Polítics de Catalunya*, p. 54.

[8] Miquel Caminal, *Nacionalisme i Partits Nacionals a Catalunya* (Barcelona: Empúries, 1998), p. 163.

[9] Marcet and Argelaguet, 'Nationalist parties in Catalonia', p. 75.

[10] Marcet and Argelaguet, 'Nationalist parties in Catalonia', p. 74.

[11] Centro de Investigaciones Sociológicas. Study no. 2,199, Nov.–Dec. 1995, quoted in Marcet and Argelaguet, 'Nationalist parties in Catalonia', p. 80.

[12] Jordi Pujol in a speech to the CDC Congress, November, 1996, quoted in Caminal, *Nacionalisme i Partits Nacionals a Catalunya*, p. 178.

[13] Caminal, *Nacionalisme i Partits Nacionals a Catalunya*, pp. 174–176.

[14] G. Colomé, 'El Partit dels Socialistes de Catalunya', in J-M Maravall et al., *Los Partidos Socialistas en Europa* (Barcelona: ICPS, 1994), pp. 43–44.

[15] Colomé, 'El Partit dels Socialistes de Catalunya', p. 51.

[16] Soler Llebaria, 'Las elecciones autonómicas en Cataluña (1980–1995)', p. 233.

[17] Molas, *Diccionari dels Partits Polítics de Catalunya*, p. 242.

[18] Caminal, *Nacionalisme i Partits Nacionals a Catalunya*, p. 170.

[19] Centro de Investigaciones Sociológicas. Study no. 2,199, Nov.–Dec. 1995, quoted in Marcet and Argelaguet, 'Nationalist parties in Catalonia', p. 80.

[20] Caminal, *Nacionalisme i Partits Nacionals a Catalunya*, pp. 185–186.

[21] PSC party documents, *Per Catalunya. Ara, un nou Federalisme, www.psc.es/catala/docs/htm.*

[22] Ibid.

[23] Ibid.

[24] Marcet and Argelaguet, 'Nationalist parties in Catalonia', p. 84.

[25] Ibid.

[26] J. Argelaguet *et al.*, 'Anàlisi sociològica dels assistents al XIX Congrès Nacional d'ERC (Barcelona, 1993)', *Papers*, 54, 1998, 187–200.

[27] Marcet and Argelaguet, 'Nationalist parties in Catalonia', p. 83.

[28] ERC party documents, *www.erc-cat.org/pagines/historia2.html.*

[29] Marcet and Argelaguet, , 'Nationalist parties in Catalonia', p. 83.

[30] Soler Llebaria, 'Las elecciones autonómicas en Cataluña (1980–1995)', p. 248.

[31] Soler Llebaria, 'Las elecciones autonómicas en Cataluña (1980–1995)', p. 244.

[32] Marcet and Argelaguet, 'Nationalist parties in Catalonia', p. 80.

[33] *www.erc-cat.org/pagines/historia2.html.*

[34] Caminal, *Nacionalisme i Partits Nacionals a Catalunya* , pp. 190–1.

[35] This internal struggle among the anti-Franco forces is vividly portrayed in George Orwell's *Homage to Catalonia*, and later in Ken Loach's film *Land and Freedom*.

[36] Baras and Matas, 'Els partits polítics i el sistema de partits', p. 174.

[37] IC-V party document, *Principis bàsics per a un programa d'esquerres ecosocialista en la transició al segle XXI*, approved by the 5th National Assembly of IC-V, Barcelona, November 1998. *www.ic-v.org.*

[38] *www.ic-v.org.*

[39] Caminal, *Nacionalisme i Partits Nacionals a Catalunya*, p. 168.

[40] F. Pallarès, 'Les eleccions de 1999 al parlament de Catalunya' in F. Pallarès (ed), *Les eleccions i el comportament electoral a Catalunya, 1989–1999*, (Barcelona: Ed. Mediterrània, 2000).

[41] Soler Llebaria, 'Las elecciones autonómicas en Cataluña (1980–1995)', p. 242.

[42] Caminal, *Nacionalisme i Partits Nacionals a Catalunya*, p.189.

[43] Soler Llebaria, 'Las elecciones autonómicas en Cataluña (1980–1995)', p. 242.

[44] Ibid.

4

Basque Political Parties

Francisco Letamendia

Historical Background: The Political Parties and the Security Situation in the Basque Country

The Basques are an ancient people with a unique language, occupying a territory at the western end of the Pyrenees straddling the French and Spanish borders, so that there are, in fact, two parts to the Basque Country. The southern Basque Country located on the Spanish side of the border is, however, divided politically and administratively between the Autonomous Community of the Basque Country and the Autonomous Community of Navarre, which nationalists claim as part of their territory. The Basques in Spain, as a border people occupying the border with France, have had, since the Middle Ages, privileges known as the *forals* or the right to a certain fiscal independence, which lasted into the modern period but were abolished by the Franco regime.

The Basques thus developed a strong sense of identity based on their linguistic uniqueness, the mystery surrounding their origins, and their special position within the mediaeval Spanish monarchies.[1] At the end of the 19th century, they differentiated themselves from the rest of Spain because of the high degree of industrialization in the region. This attracted Spanish immigrants who settled in the cities, joining socialist and trade union movements, while traditional Basque society was faithful to the Catholic Church.[2] The arrival of these immigrants from other parts of Spain worried early Basque nationalists such as Sabino Arana, the founder of the Basque Nationalist Party (PNV – *Partido Nacionalista Vasco*) in 1896, who formulated the early doctrine of Basque nationalism in terms more racist than linguistic or cultural and was quite opposed to the intermingling of Basques and others. Fortunately, this aspect of Arana's doctrine was quietly abandoned by later nationalists.[3] Nevertheless, Basque nationalism offers an interesting contrast to Catalonia where the emphasis is much more on culture and language as identity markers.[4]

During the Spanish Civil War, the majority of Basques of all political tendencies opposed Franco.[5] In the 1960s, the PNV re-emerged but some members of its youth wing founded ETA (*Euskadi ta Askatasuna* – Basque Homeland and Freedom in Basque) in 1959. ETA was a coalition of different groups some of which emphasized political actions, while others were more inclined to military action. We can thus distinguish three political 'blocs' in the Basque Country at the time of the transition to democracy (1976–8): a moderate nationalist bloc represented by the PNV; a radical nationalist bloc represented by the various groups emanating from ETA such as *Herri Batasuna*, created in early 1978; and a pro-Spanish bloc, represented by the Spanish political parties such as the Spanish Socialist Workers' Party (*Partido Socialista Obrero Español* – PSOE or Socialists) or the right-wing parties such as the UCD (now defunct) and the Popular Alliance (*Alianza Popular* – AP) which would later become the Popular Party (*Partido Popular* – PP), and attracting supporters either from the working-class constituencies of non-Basque origin[6] or from some sections of the industrial and financial bourgeoisie.

The moderate nationalists of the PNV have ruled the Basque Autonomous Community since its inception in 1980, sometimes alone, sometimes in coalition with the Basque Socialist Party (*Partido Socialista de Euskadi* – PSE–PSOE). Most Basque nationalists, however, are unenthusiastic about the 1978 constitutional settlement which, in their eyes, divided the southern Basque Country by creating two separate Communities and did not go far enough in recognizing its national character. Another source of dissatisfaction has been the failure to implement fully the *foral* laws which would allow the Basques to gain control over their fiscal and tax regimes.[7] Basques feel they pay too much to the central government to subsidize the southern Spanish ACs.[8] Even more intense has been the conflict between the PNV and the various radical nationalist groups clustering around ETA and *Herri Batasuna* (Popular Unity – HB). But radical nationalists have also been bitterly divided into different factions.[9]

The radical nationalists succeeded throughout the 1980s in shaping the political agenda of the Basque Country and, to some extent, of Spain itself.[10] This provoked a repressive response from the Spanish state which sometimes used its own anti-terrorist organisations of dubious legality, such as the Anti-terrorist Liberation Groups (*Grupos*

Antiterroristas de Liberación – GAL), responsible for more than 25 deaths.[11] By the mid 1990s, however, ETA was in a position similar to that reached by the Provisional IRA in the mid 1980s – it could only disrupt the system but could not achieve a positive outcome of any of its declared aims. In order words, it could not go forward politically but neither could it abandon the armed struggle. This was especially important as there was a considerable number of prisoners in different parts of Spain outside the Basque Country. To give up the armed struggle would have seemed like abandoning them. Nevertheless, by the 1990s, it was clear to many Basques that nationalists needed to go beyond the armed struggle.

Richard Gillespie lists five factors which led to the 1998 cease-fire: political setbacks experienced by ETA and HB; decline in ETA's military capacity with more members in prison than active outside; isolation of the militarists from the mainstream of Basque society; generational change in which younger militants were less convinced by the old Marxist discourse; the changing international context, especially Europe and the Irish peace process; and, finally, developments within Basque nationalism as a whole. Gillespie also points to the influence of the Irish peace process and the close links between Sinn Fein and HB which encouraged the latter to follow a similar path.[12]

Even before the 1998 ceasefire, the Ajuria–Enea Agreement (1988–98) sought the full implementation of the Basque Autonomous Statute as a solution to the national conflict, as well the negotiation of an anti-terrorist agreement. This failed basically because of the difficulty of reconciling those who believed in democracy and those who used violence. A second attempt was the Lizarra Agreement (September 1998) agreed among nationalists which sought to negotiate in terms of the Basque Country's relationship with Spain. This was not welcomed by the parties to the Ajuria–Enea Agreement, and this gave credibility to the interpretations of the absent centralist parties, who saw the agreement as a way of promoting Basque nationalism. This led to the emergence of an anti-nationalist counter-movement which was, in turn, fed by the ongoing low-intensity violence (*kale borroka*) aimed almost exclusively at these anti-nationalist protagonists. The rejection by the PP government in Madrid of any strategy that was conciliatory strengthened the negative position of the MLNV (the Basque National Liberation Movement) towards the Lizarra Agreement, and the MLNV eventually turned against the other parties to the Agreement. The straw that broke the Agreement's back was ETA's breach of the ceasefire. The third agreement was the *Partido Popular-Partido Socialista Obrero Español* (PP-PSOE) Pact for Freedom and against Terrorism (December 2000), which was an explicitly anti-terrorist agreement but lacked any plan for resolving the conflict. The Pact was opposed to violence, but also attacked Basque sovereignty, which was accused of denying freedom to parts of the Basque Country.

The Political Parties in the Basque Country

Party membership is high in the Autonomous Community (AC), with some 66,000 people active in the various parties. Current membership numbers are estimated as follows:

Table 4:0: Numbers of political party members in the Basque Country

PNV:	31,000
PSE-Euskadiko Ezkerra (PSE-EE):	10,000
Batasuna (former HB):	12,000
PP:	4,000
EA:	15,000
EB-IU:	5,000
Unidad Alavesa (UA):	1,000

Key:

EA:	Eusko Alkartasuna (Basque Solidarity)
Batasuna (Unity):	formerly Herri Batasuna
EB-IU:	Izquierda Unida-Ezker Batua
	(United Left-Basque Unity)
PSE-EE:	Partido Socialista de Euskadi-Euskadiko Ezkerra
	(Basque Socialist Party-Basque Left)
PNV:	Partido Nacionalista Vasco
	(Basque Nationalist Party)

The nationalist parties, especially PNV and EA, and indeed *Ezker Batua*, are mass parties, whereas the Basque branches of statewide parties, especially the PP, are cadre parties.[13]

Partido Nacionalista Vasco (PNV)

Historical Background and Party Ideology

The *Partido Nacionalista Vasco*, the oldest nationalist party in Europe and now over a hundred years old, led the Basque nationalist government under José Antonio Aguirre during the Civil War. After Franco's death, its congress adopted a platform that was Christian democratic and appealed to all classes. It was Basque nationalist as well as European and sought a third way between capitalism and socialism.

Party Structure and Leadership

PNV leaders have headed the Basque governments, as provided for in the Statute of Autonomy, without a break since the first elections for autonomous governments were held in 1980. A single party government headed by Garaikoetxea lasted until 1984. Ardanza subsequently headed either one-party governments, based on a coalition programme (1984–8), or coalition governments, with the Socialist Party as a virtually permanent partner.

After the 1985–6 split which resulted in the formation of EA, the PNV did not suffer any leadership problems for a long time. Xavier Arzalluz, re-elected president of the EBB (*Euskadi Buru Batzar* or PNV executive) by the Assembly for the sixth time in December 1995, was the undisputed and charismatic party leader. A new generation of 'chiefs' (*burukides*) led by Egibar won office in Gipuzkoa (Guipúzcoa) province and in Bizkaia (Vizcaya) they shared power with the older generation.

Electoral Performance and Profile

The Lizarra Pact of September 1998 gave the PNV an electoral advantage in the elections for the autonomous government at the end of that year, and the PNV formed a new coalition government with EA, led by Juan José Ibarretxe. In 1999, *Euzkal Herritarok* (EH) signed an agreement to enter government which gave the ruling nationalist parties an absolute majority in the Basque parliament.

ETA broke its truce in November 1999, complaining that the PNV and EA had not honoured their promises on the national question. With effect from 2000, after the first attack which resulted in fatalities,

he government agreement was broken. When EH left the Basque
parliament, the Ibarretxe government became a minority one. PP and
PSOE pressure forced early elections to be held in May 2001, which
he PNV-EA coalition again won. A government was formed with a
new coalition which, besides the PNV-EA, now included the left-wing
IU-Ezker Batua.

The PNV-EA won the April 2005 regional elections but only by a small
margin, losing their overall majority. PNV-EA won twenty-nine out of
seventy-five seats (four fewer than in the previous elections). With a minority
government, Ibarretxe would have to rely on the Basque Communist
Party votes to push his policies through a regional parliament.

Figure 4.1: Number of PNV votes polled from 1986 to 2005

1986A:	286,000
1990A:	289,000
1991M:	297,000
1993G:	286,000
1994E:	233,000
1994A:	303,000
1995M:	310,000
1996G:	314,000
1998A:	396,000
2000G:	347,000
2001A:	599,000 or 33 seats (PNV+EA)
2003M:	497,000 (PNV+EA)
2005A:	29 seats (38.6%) (PNV+EA)

A =	for Autonomous Community assembly
E=	for European Parliament
G =	General elections (to Spanish *Cortes*)
M=	Municipal elections

The PNV and the Autonomic State

One of the fruits of the alliance between the PNV and the Socialist
Party was the Ajuria–Enea Pact of 1988, signed by all the Basque
constitutional parties, which had two aims: containing ETA's violence
and HB's radical nationalism, and strengthening the Statute of
Autonomy. In 1992, talks between the PNV and HB on opening up a
peace process broke down. From 1993 onwards, the PNV and its

periodic partner in government, EA, felt more and more hampered by
the fact that, thanks to the statewide parties which had signed it, the
pact had become a mere instrument for attacking ETA-MLNV and
was not fulfilling its aim of further implementation of the powers
contained in the 1979 Gernika (Guernica) Statute.

The Basque government realized that the transfer of powers was
still subordinate to the political interests of the government party in
Madrid. In 1980 and 1981 there had been a major transfer of powers,
to underpin the autonomous government at a time when there was a
major offensive by ETA and political instability in Spain. The transfers,
carried out in 1985 and 1987, were a response to the government
programme of the PNV-PSE; but no transfer of powers took place
between 1988 and 1993. All the Basque political parties involved in the
Ajuria–Enea Pact agreed in 1993 on the criteria for the transfer to the
Basque Country of fifty-four further powers, including economic
affairs and industrial relations. But in 1994, the socialist government
promised to transfer only eight or nine of them, none of which was
very important. The coalition government of PNV, EA and PSE formed
after the 1994 elections was under great pressure, stemming from the
continued blocking of the transfer of new powers, from the differences
which emerged around the Concierto[14] (the main tool of Basque
fiscal policy) and from debates between EA, which thought that the
Ajuria–Enea Pact entitled it to include the right to self-determination
in its remit, and the statewide parties, who had an opposing inter-
pretation of the Pact.

From 1995 onwards, some parts of the PNV leadership, availing
themselves of the cover provided by the *Elkarri* initiatives, embarked
on a new path towards peace.[15] This path, which involved moving
closer to HB and seeking an 'open-ended dialogue' on the resolution
of the Basque conflict, would give the PNV an indirect way of
developing the powers contained in the autonomy statute, a process
which seemed to be increasingly obstructed by the dynamics of the
Ajuria–Enea Pact. This is how the so-called 'Ollora theses' came to be
revealed during a peace conference organized by *Elkarri* in 1995. The
essence of these is that the Basque conflict is political by nature; that
any peace process must recognize that both sides have a legitimate
political position; that the PNV would be ready to continue dialogue
with ETA and MLNV and to support a reform of the constitution
that recognized the right to self-determination and would set in
motion a move towards sovereignty that would lead to peace.

The replacement of the PSOE in central government by the PP did not change Madrid's position on the Basque Country in some respects, while, in other respects, there was a significant shift. The PP proved receptive to PNV demands on fiscal policy and concluded an agreement in 1997 on the Basque Economic Concert, strengthened by the PP-PNV investiture pact of 1996. But the PP hardened its line on the peace process, refusing, inter alia, the agreements on the reinsertion into society of Basque prisoners that had been reached in the Ajuria–Enea Pact. In 1996 the Ollora theses became the basis of the official PNV position. The PNV document of February 1997 on the peace process turned 'open-ended dialogue' into official policy.

After the May 2001 elections the programme of the winning PNV-EA coalition was based on the three-point peace process (see above), dialogue between all protagonists and self-government, and had taken on board the sovereignist principles of the Lizarra declaration, whereby the Basque people were to decide its destiny; but the cabinet was wary of an agreement that had been reached by a number of protagonists outside parliament and wanted to protect itself from any changes of mood on ETA's part. It therefore proposed to set down its proposals in the form of a bill that would be debated exclusively within parliament. The parliament set up a Commission on Self-Government, which reported in July 2002.

Based on this, the Basque government took a year to prepare a bill, which it tabled in the Basque parliament in October 2003. The bill, entitled 'Proposed New Statute for the Euskadi Community' (known as the Ibarretxe Plan) was inspired by the experience of Quebec, with its twin pillars of 'sovereignty-association' and a referendum. The territory of the Basque Community is defined as the three provinces of the current Autonomous Community, which might establish relations with Navarre and Iparralde.[16] If Basque citizens wish to change their relationship to the Spanish state, Basque and Spanish institutions must negotiate the structure and form such changes should take. The Basque parliament decided to proceed with this bill, though it was not at first passed.

PSOE considered this unconstitutional, as the bill questioned the idea of a single Spanish national sovereignty as set down in the constitution (see the Introduction to this book). The PP appealed formally to the constitutional court to suspend work on the bill and, using its Senate majority, rushed through a law that would punish anyone calling a referendum outside the constitution with a sentence of three to five years.

The PNV gave firm support to the Ibarretxe government's plans, as a strategic objective, but was divided on the separate question of what alliances to seek. When Arzalluz stepped down of his own accord, the PNV leadership elections pitted two candidates against each other. Joseba Egibar was in favour of alliances with the sovereignists, while Josu Jon Imaz, now spokesperson for the Basque government, stood for a policy of compromise with the centre.

On 30 December 2004 the Basque parliament voted in favour of the Ibarretxe Plan by a very small majority, which included the vote of MPs from the by now outlawed HB. In accordance with the constitution, the plan was submitted to the *Cortes*, with Ibarretxe supporting it in person on 1 February 2005. Predictably it was crushed by the votes of the statewide parties PP and PSOE, receiving only 29 votes in favour and 313 against. The PNV's strategy had thus run into a brick wall, and its leaders faced the prospect of going ahead with an illegal referendum, which, at best, might scrape a very small majority among Basque voters.[17]

Ibarretxe had made it clear that the Basque regional elections held on 17 April 2005 would be a test of the Basque population's support for his Plan and that if the Basques gave him their vote in these elections they would in effect be endorsing the Ibarretxe Plan. The results of this election, with the PNV-EA alliance winning only by a small margin with twenty-nine out of seventy-five seats (four seats fewer than in the 2001 elections), were therefore a blow to the Ibarretxe Plan and were disappointing from the point of view of the PNV-EA Basque nationalist alliance. The results of the April 2005 AC elections are also discussed in further detail at the end of the chapter.

Eusko Alkartasuna (EA)

Historical Background and Party Ideology

Eusko Alkartasuna (EA – meaning Basque Solidarity) was created in 1986 out of a split in the PNV caused by a number of conflicts: between Arzalluz and Garaikoetxea over the leadership; between the traditional view of the PNV, which held that the institutional model for the Basque Country should be decentralized along the lines of the historic territories, and the EA's view that such a model should be centralized; between the centre-left position of EA on foreign policy, moral questions and social and economic policy and the more centrist line of the PNV; and finally between EA's explicit defence of the right to self-determination as the modern approach to sovereignty and PNV's historic conception, based on historic rights (*fueros*).

Electoral Performance

The EA became a member of the 1990–1 autonomous government coalition (PNV-EA-EE) and after 1995 became a permanent member of the coalition governments. EA entered into the Ibarretxe government in 1998. Since 2001 the EA has formed stable electoral coalitions with the PNV, having the same number of ministers (three) in both Ibarretxe governments.

The results of the April 2005 AC elections are discussed in the PNV section above and at the end of the chapter.

Figure 4.2: Number of EA votes polled from 1986 to 2005

1986A:	181,000
1990A:	115,000
1991M:	118,000
1993G:	117,000
1994E:	78,000
1994A:	104,000
1995M:	118,000
1996G:	103,000
1998A:	108,000
2000G:	86,000
2001A:	599,000 or 33 seats (PNV+EA)
2003M:	497,000 (PNV+EA)
2005A:	29 seats (38.6%) (PNV+EA)

A =	for Autonomous Community assembly
E=	for European Parliament
G =	General elections (to Spanish *Cortes*)
M=	Municipal elections

Party Structure and Leadership

Garaikoetxea's withdrawal from the leadership resulted in the election of a unity team to the leadership at the 4th congress of 2000 (Begoña Errazti as president and Gorka Knorr as secretary general), with the support of 65 per cent of the membership. EA has been exploring the possibility of setting up a network of left-wing nationalist parties opposed to violence, and in April 2002 signed the Bayona pact with the leftist group from Navarre, *Batzarre* (a split from *Batasuna Aralar*) and *Abertzaleen Batasuna* from Iparralde, which drew angry criticism from ETA. In EA's 5th congress of November 2003, Errazti, the centrist candidate for the presidency, backed by Garaikoetxea, clashed with Galdós from the moderate wing, who favoured strengthening links with the PNV, and Intxaurraga, from the left of the party, who championed the Bayona pact. Despite the alliance between the first two groups, the left-wing opposition in the party took 40 per cent of the vote, compared to 60 per cent for Errazti, who was re-elected president.

EA and the Autonomic State

From the time of its membership of the 1990–1 autonomous government coalition (PNV-EA-EE) and especially since becoming a permanent member of the coalition governments after 1995, EA's line regarding Basque independence softened, while at the same time its discourse on self-determination made headway within the PNV. Unity of action in parliament lasted barely a year from 1992 to 1993, with the split of *Euskal Ezkerra* from *Euskadiko Ezkerra* (see below). In its 4th congress of 1995, EA proclaimed renewed support for 'a united, in-dependent Basque state' and argued within the Ajuria–Enea Pact meetings for pursuing the second phase of the pact, namely developing the powers contained in the statute. It also argued that the right to self-determination be accepted explicitly by the pact steering committee. Failure to accept its position led EA into involvement with any project likely to suggest an alternative to the pact.

   The undisputed leadership of Carlos Garaikoetxea, who has been the party's main electoral asset, has not prevented considerable tension between its radical and moderate wings. In 1998, 40 per cent of the activists refused to support candidates put up by the party.

   EA's entry into the Ibarretxe government in 1998, together with the fact that any leftward expansion is limited by the presence of radical nationalism, has blurred the party's image in recent years. Starting from a lower position, EA has gone down the same route as the PNV, so far as the Lizarra experiment is concerned. It is criticized by ETA in the same breath as the majority party.

Partido Socialista de Euskadi – Euskadiko Ezkerra (PSE-EE)

Historical Backgound and Party Ideology

The Basque Country's oldest party, the Socialist Party, has strong roots, especially in the industrial zones of Vizcaya and Guipúzcoa where it has had *Casas de Pueblo* since the last quarter of the nineteenth century.[18] During the Second Republic it was a member of the Basque National Unity Government and was attacked by Franco. It was subsequently a member of the Basque government in exile, but its renaming as the PSE (Socialist Party of Euskadi) dates from after Franco's death. Its radical discourse on Basque social and national issues between 1975 and 1977 was to undergo a change, parallel to that of the statewide party PSOE, as debates on the constitution progressed. Since 1979 the PSE has consistently stood up for the constitution and the autonomy statute. By way of adapting to the territorial organization of the ACs, the party's remit has been further divided since the early 1980s, with the Socialist Party of Navarre (PSN) splitting off from the PSE.

The collapse of the *Unión de Centro Democrático* (UCD) after taking office in 1982 and the electoral weakness of the Spanish right made the PSOE the party which provided some national backbone to a Spain made up of autonomous communities. To a far greater extent than the *Partit dels Socialistes de Catalunya* (PSC), the PSE has bought into the centralizing logic of its mother party (technically it is a *federación* or branch of PSOE), helped also no doubt by the continuing political violence of ETA.

Party Structure, Leadership and Electoral Performance

It has, at any rate, enjoyed considerable success at the polls for over a decade. Txiki Benegas led the PSE from 1977 to 1988, and Ramón Jáuregui for another decade until 1997. The latter had to overcome the hard-line centralism of García Damborenea, the strong man of Vizcaya, who quit the party in 1990.

1992 saw what was a merger in legal terms, but in practice the take-over, of *Euskadiko Ezkerra*, the party which was heir to the vanished ETA-PM (ETA-Político-Militar) and which had supported the constitution since the late 1980s. The increased vote in the 1993 general election was seen as a result of the merger by the PSE-EE. This was the period in which 'post-nationalism' was talked up and claimed to be a modern, inclusive project, compared to Basque nationalism, which was presented as archaic and exclusive. There was also an attempt at a 'pro-Basque policy' inspired by the old leader of EE Mario Onaindia, which was short-lived because of lack of support from the statewide party. At the 33rd PSOE congress of 1994, the apparent triumph of Felipe González's modernizers over the followers of Alfonso Guerra merely disguised the ever-growing influence of the party's regional barons who rule the ACs in southern Spain and who dominate PSOE congresses with their votes and delegates. Basque socialism, however, cut a modest figure on this scene, managing only to get Jáuregui onto the national executive. The 2nd congress of the PSE-EE was held a month later in April. The party reverted to its earlier line, proclaiming its 'loyalty to the autonomy statute'.

What distinguishes the PSE-EE from the PSOE is that its sub-groups are defined by the different ways that its members deal with Basque nationalism in different territories. The territorial executives elected in 1994 were of a different complexion. In Guipúzcoa, Eguiguren, who represents a progressive, pro-nationalist politics, won. In Alava, it was Buesa, a hard-line anti-nationalist. In Vizcaya, Redondo Terreros, who tried to stick to a middle-of-the-road position, just scraped in. In 1994–5 the *Osakidetza* scandal made the news. The socialist former directors of the Basque health service had been operating a scam for years in the field of public employment, fiddling exam results so that some 350 candidates with PSE links obtained posts. The position of Ramón Jáuregui, who was criticized by party activists for not accepting responsibility for this, was weakened.

A falling vote in the 1994 autonomous elections led to the 'pro-Basque' line being changed. 1995 was the PSOE's *annus horribilis*; news leaked out of the implication of some leading lights of the socialist government in the GAL death squads, and the judicial inquiry began into the FILESA organization for illegal financial activity.[19] The possibility began to dawn, reinforced by the European elections of 1994, that the PP might take over government from the PSOE. Fear of a right-wing victory helped keep up the socialist vote in the 1996 general election.

The increasing power of socialist barons from the south was demonstrated forcefully in the 34th PSOE congress of 1997. Felipe González resigned, having failed to reduce the size of the party executive. An expanded executive commission made room for the territorial barons, and Almunia, elected as secretary general, was the link between Felipe's supporters in the party and the new socialist powerbrokers.

The 3rd PSE-EE Congress in 1997 saw Jáuregui step down and the old coalition of Vizcaya and Alava socialists replaced by one between Vizcaya and Guipúzcoa. Redondo Terreros was elected secretary-general with the backing of Eguiguren in an executive which by now had virtually no traces of the old *Euskadiko Ezkerra*. The primary elections for candidacies to the party presidency and the autonomous institutions, which were approved by the 34th congress, were the channel through which grassroots disquiet with the leadership was expressed. Borrell, standing for the presidency against the official candidate Almunia, won in April 1998 thanks more to members' resentment of the party machine than to his 'Jacobin' programme. In primaries for the party lists for elections to the various ACs, Redondo, the official candidate in the Basque country, beat the alternative Jacobin candidate, Rosa Díez, only by a small margin.

Borrell's intention to break with the past clashed with the firm line of defence of the old socialist officials who had been condemned for their implication in the GAL death squads. This line was inspired by the actual party leadership, and González had given it his backing. The PSE-EE, which was weak within the party at large and had no real support on the national executive, had to swallow some decisions taken by the central leadership, for instance their withdrawal from the Basque government in June 1998, in response to the vote by all the nationalist parties, including HB, against members of parliament in the ACs having to take an oath of loyalty to the constitution. Another example was the inclusion of the socialist barons from the south and their aggressive anti-nationalist campaign in the elections to the ACs in October 1998.

Figure 4.3: Number of PSE-EE votes polled from 1986 to 2005

1986A:	252,000
1990A:	202,000
1991M:	193,000
1993G:	291,000
1994E:	165,000
1994A:	173,000
1995M:	188,000
1996G:	295,000
1998A:	218,000
2000G:	266,000
2001A:	250,000 r 13 seats
2003M:	250,000
2005A:	18 seats (22.6%)

A =	for Autonomous Community assembly
E =	for European Parliament
G =	General elections (to Spanish *Cortes*)
M =	Municipal elections

The results of the April 2005 AC elections are discussed in further detail later in the chapter.

PSE-EE and the Autonomic State

After the Lizarra declaration, the PSE-EE under Redondo took a more centralizing line, characterized by the refusal to take account of any of the possibilities for dialogue offered by Lizarra and by the growing hope that a PSE-EE/PP governing majority could be put together, especially after the formation of the Ibarretxe government. The leadership crisis of Spanish socialism handed the PP an absolute majority in the general election of March 2000. Rodríguez Zapatero's election as secretary general of the PSOE in July was meant to resolve that crisis. The ideological sources of inspiration for the new leader and his team are communitarianism and republicanism. Within this discourse, he accepts the concept of a plural Spain but maintains that this plural Spain does not imply any sharing of the Spanish state's sovereignty and therefore rules out the 'sovereignism' which is the choice of the majority of Basques. This attitude has doubtless been reinforced by the attacks which have claimed the lives of socialist activists since ETA broke its truce, with four fatalities in 2000 and 2001. The Antiterrorist Pact between the PP and PSOE in December 2000 was a socialist initiative in reply to ETA's assassination of the Catalan socialist and ex-minister Lluch.

The 4th congress of the PSE-EE re-elected Nicolás Redondo as secretary general, but the new leadership only drew the support of 51 per cent of delegates. Redondo persuaded the PSE-EE to echo the centralist line of PP leader Mayor Oreja, hoping to win a centralist majority in the AC elections of May 2001.

Failure to achieve this goal was critical for Redondo's strategy. In autumn 2001, a 'pro-Basque' platform emerged, inspired by activists from Guipúzcoa like Eguiguren. This platform accepted the existence of conflict in the Basque country, refused self-determination but accepted a referendum for the Basque people held under democratic conditions, in line with the provisions of the Canadian Supreme Court as regards self-determination in Quebec. It also accepted the principle of shared sovereignty. Redondo resigned in December 2001, and his successors were beaten at the 5th PSE-EE congress in March 2002, winning only 34 per cent of the votes. The centrist Patxi López took over as leader.

However, PP political and media pressure prevented Spanish socialists from distancing themselves from centralizing attitudes which excluded radical Basque nationalism and were hostile to the governing variety. The PSOE shared PP hostility to the Ibarretxe government's bill and reluctantly supported the 'Law on Parties' designed to make successor organizations to Herri Batasuna illegal in the Spanish parliament.

In August 2003 the PSOE published a paper on subnational government which defines its concept of a 'plural Spain' within the model of the State of Autonomous Communities. It talks about a reform of the Spanish senate, to turn it into a forum which would guarantee the ACs' participation in influencing the state's will, and the reform of all the AC statutes, except for the Basque one. It goes along with the PSE-EE's motto of 'more of the statute', in other words the completion of the transfer of outstanding powers under the statute without the revision of its text. But this proposal lacks credibility, as the PSOE was in office from 1982 to 1996 and never transferred such powers during this time.

The PSC's bid to form a government in Catalonia with the left-wing nationalist party ERC, which openly supports the Ibarretxe Plan, might however have led to a shift in Spanish (and hence Basque) socialist strategy, towards a solution to the conflict inspired by the Northern Ireland model. But this was unlikely to happen before the general election of March 2004, since any moves in this direction would be presented by PP spin doctors as proof that the Socialists were 'traitors' to Spanish unity. When in March 2004 the PSC and left-wing nationalists did win at the polls and formed a government, it did not seem as if PSOE thinking had changed very much, certainly if the party's *Cortes* vote on the Ibarretxe Plan (see above) is anything to go by.

The Partido Popular (PP)

Historical Background

The short history of the Basque Popular Party is personified by Mayor Oreja. After a previous phase of restructuring of the Spanish right within the Basque country that began in 1987, the Basque PP began life in 1990, the year in which the national PP was founded. It got off to a bad start, as many of its Alava members split off to form *Unidad Alavesa* (UA).

Party Leadership and Electoral Performance

The PP's progress across Spain in the general election of 1993 and the European election of 1994 helped consolidate the Basque PP and bring it to its peak. Its regional congress in 1993 set out the model of leadership which the party has kept, with the tandem of Mayor Oreja as president and undisputed party leader, and Iturgaiz as his secretary and right-hand man.

The 22nd PP congress in January 1996 confirmed Aznar's authority and rewarded Mayor Oreja with a post as one of the party's vice-presidents. After the PP's electoral win of that year, Mayor Oreja was appointed interior minister in the Spanish government.

Once the PP had put behind it the short-term crisis of early 2003, caused by its disastrous handling of the oil slick from the sunken tanker *Prestige* and Spanish participation in the highly unpopular Iraq war, all the polls suggested a further triumph for the party in the general election of March 2004.

Yet Mayor Oreja's star is on the wane. He is perceived in the Basque Country as caring little about Basque affairs. The Basque government's budget estimates, heavily amended by the PP, got through by one vote only – his own, as he was absent from the chamber when the vote was taken. The PP's successive failures to shift Basque nationalism out of government in the AC have put him in a corner in Madrid, where the candidate for prime minister was not him but Mariano Rajoy. If the power vacuum that has been created has not had greater consequences in the Basque country, this is due to the Basque PP's lack of autonomy vis-à-vis Madrid. A nucleus of power does exist in Alava, the least nationalist province in the AC, embodied in the two PP leaders who won office in the 1999 and 2003 municipal elections, Rabanera, Speaker of the Alava assembly and Alonso, mayor of Gasteiz (Vitoria).

Figure 4.4: Number of PP votes polled from 1986 to 2005

1986A:	56,000
1990A:	83,000
1991M:	76,000
1993G:	175,000
1994E:	158,000
1994A:	146,000
1995M:	160,000
1996G:	229,000
1998A:	250,000
2000G:	323,000
2001A:	232,000 or 19 seats (PP+UA)
2003M:	212,000
2005A:	15 seats (17.3%)

A =	for Autonomous Community assembly
E=	for European Parliament
G =	General elections (to Spanish *Cortes*)
M=	Municipal elections

The results of the April 2005 AC elections are discussed in further detail later in the chapter.

The PP and the Autonomic State

Mayor Oreja's period of uncontested authority over the Basque PP would lead some of the party's activists to see the Basque problem as one of security. This explains the divergence between the Basque PP and the other parties in the Ajuria–Enea Pact over the peace process, defence by the Basque PP of the transfer of prisoners to remote corners of Spain (which was in fact illegal) and the creation of difficulties by the Basque PP over the reinsertion of prisoners into society. The Basque PP's regional congress of 1996 elected Iturgaiz as president. The provincial party executives which were formed a month later would face problems of law and order in Guipúzcoa.

The killing of the Guipúzcoa leader Ordóñez in January 1995 was the first of a series of attacks on PP councillors, which intensified through 1997 and 1998. Mayor Oreja advocated in 1997 a 'joint project' with the democratic Basque parties, aimed at stifling the MLNV politically and within civil society. The cruel death of councillor Miguel Angel Blanco a month later gave birth to the so-called 'spirit of Ermua', an example of wishful thinking, which allowed the PP to believe its project to be feasible. This line, to which the PP stuck unwaveringly until ETA's declaration of an indefinite ceasefire in September 1998, made the party the repository of the 'Spanish vote' in the Basque country, taking over this role from the socialists.

During the long ETA ceasefire from September 1998 to November 1999, the PP government made no gestures suggesting a willingness to further the peace process. It did not bring prisoners back to serve their sentences in Basque prisons (of some 600 Basque prisoners, only fifty are serving their time in local prisons). It did not have more than one meeting with ETA spokespeople outside Spain (indeed some of the latter were arrested by the French police immediately afterwards). It would not begin any dialogue on the Basque political situation with the parties which had signed Lizarra, arguing that 'peace cannot come with a price attached to it'. This narrow-mindedness, which resulted in the end of the ETA ceasefire, paid off in Spanish politics, where the PP won an absolute majority in the general election of March 2000. The PP hardened up the wording of the PP-PSOE pact of December 2000 (For Freedom and against Terrorism), by implying that Basque nationalism as a whole bore some intellectual and moral responsibility for terrorism.

The Basque PP, which is a party of elites like its Spanish equivalent, is linked to the figure of its leader, Mayor Oreja, whom the hard-line centralists were pushing as a candidate for the premiership, once Aznar announced his retirement. Prior to the AC elections of May 2001 Mayor Oreja managed to win over the Basque socialist party, led by Redondo, to his viewpoint and he gave financial backing to associations of victims of terrorism and centralist think-tanks such as the *Ermua Forum, Basta Ya*, or *Fundación para la Libertad*, in which groups of academics, many of them from a socialist background, made a name for themselves. They combined condemnation of terrorism, as one might expect, with a high degree of hostility to Basque nationalism and firm opposition to any changes in the Spanish legal or political framework.

9/11 in New York brought about a rock-hard alliance – political, ideological and military – between Bush's conservative republicanism, with its one-dimensional view of the world, and Aznar's party. The PP has, in the view of some critics, revived a sociological version of Francoism, which seeks to reconstruct Spanish national unity against an internal enemy personified by Basque nationalism as a whole. It is abetted by a judiciary which is favourably disposed to its plans. The 14th PP congress of February 2002 proclaimed the principle of 'constitutional patriotism', identified with defence of the centre against Basque nationalism, as the guiding principle of party strategy.[20] Inspired by the PP, which presented the PSOE with a fait accompli, a Law on Parties was approved in spring 2002. Designed for use against *Herri Batasuna* (which then renamed itself *Batasuna* but still remained illegal) and its successors, it raised the sentence for terrorist offences to forty years in jail and, to complete the package, forbade Basque prisoners to follow programmes of study at the University of the Basque Country (in Bilbao). The judiciary criminalized anyone who had been a leader of *Batasuna* or its successor-groups in the past fifteen years. The Supreme Court prosecuted the speaker of the Basque parliament, Juan María Atutxa, for refusing to dissolve the radical group of MPs, *Socialista Abertzaleak*, on grounds that the Basque parliament was sovereign. The referendum projected in the Ibarretxe Plan sought protection against a law carrying a three to five year sentence for anyone organizing a referendum (in this case the head of the Basque government).

Unidad Alavesa (UA)

Historical Background and Party Ideology

UA was born in January 1990 when the then president of the PP in Alava, Pablo Mosquera, left the PP with a majority of members of the party executive in Alava.

The reason was the group's disagreement with the actions of Jaime Mayor Oreja who had been sent from Madrid with the task of re-organizing the PP in Euskadi. UA fed on the grievances, real or imagined, of the political class in Alava vis-à-vis nationalism but more directly on the discontent of parts of the Alava population, both Basque and immigrant, with the way that the nationalist government ran affairs in the AC, and in particular with policies applied within the historic territory of Alava. This local discontent developed into a new political project based on assertion of historic rights (*fueros*), which did not hide its sympathy for a similar project that had seen the light of day in the neighbouring Navarre AC a decade before and which called into question the institutional architecture of the Basque AC. The UA's identifying markers as a party were forged in opposition to Basque nationalism.

Electoral Performance and Internal Divisions

UA made a major breakthrough in the territory of Alava in the fourth AC elections of 1990, taking 14,034 votes (11.14 per cent and three seats in the Basque parliament).

Ever since, the party's history has been plagued by some celebrated internal divisions. The worst crisis was around 1997, though its roots go back further. The results in the 1995 local lections had led to a feeling of disenchantment in the party, which had hoped to come first in Alava. The 3rd congress in July of that year revealed two factions in conflict within the party. In 1997 R. Garín, who had been the party's deputy secretary general, openly criticized the municipal pact between UA and the PNV in Vitoria town hall. Garín resigned as deputy secretary general but kept his post as party spokesman in the provincial assembly. By March, UA was on the verge of a split, but the prospects of making progress in the AC elections of 1998 calmed things down for a while. The crisis would be resolved with the celebration of the party's seventh birthday. A report entitled 'Ideological Refoundation' was supposed to unify both factions. But the conflict worsened in August after the PSE was thrown out of the governing majority in Vitoria town hall, making UA the only partner of the PNV. The party executive then decided to table a censure motion against the PNV leader of the provincial executive, Ormazábal. Garín was against this, as he understood that it was impossible to be in coalition with the PNV in Vitoria while trying to boycott the PNV government in the provincial assembly. The majority faction in UA then embarked on a strategy of isolating Garín, while Mosquera summoned an extraordinary congress in October to solve once and for all the party's internal crisis. In this congress, the UA-PNV pact was endorsed, and critics of it were asked to resign their seats in the Basque parliament and Alava provincial assembly. On October 27, Garín and twenty-three other critics left the party for good, keeping their seats and joining a cross-party group.

The above disagreements and the electoral landslide triggered by the ETA ceasefire a month before the AC elections meant a loss of three seats and over 11,000 votes for UA, which went from being the second strongest political party in Alava to the fifth, with two seats in the Basque parliament. Since the Lizarra declaration and as a result of the PP's having filled all the space on the anti-nationalist right in the Basque country, UA has become irrelevant as a party.

Figure 4.5: Number of UA votes polled from 1990 to 1998

1990A:	14,351
1993G:	16,623
1994A:	27,682
1996G:	did not stand
1998A:	15,722
A =	for Autonomous Community assembly
G =	General elections (to Spanish *Cortes*)

Izquierda Unida-Ezker Batasua (IU-EB)

Historical Background

The history of IU-EB is inseparable from that of the Spanish IU in 1986. As with IU, the major force until 1993–4 was the Communist Party of Euskadi (EPK). The absorption of *Berdeak* (the Greens) in 1994 and especially of activists from pacifist organizations like Madrazo, changed things. EB's vote rose sharply, as its electoral territory extended to former *Euskadiko Ezkerra* (EE) voters disenchanted with EE's merger with the PSE.

Party Ideology and Internal Divisions

At the 4th congress in 1995, three tendencies were in competition: that of Madrazo, supported by the pro-nationalist group *Ekaitza*; the group of former leader and EPK member Enrique González and the centralizing tendency of Doñate. The victory of Madrazo gave a big boost again to EB in the 1996 general election. This situation gave EB some breathing space from the tensions affecting IU.

Electoral Performance

EB performed well in the 1996 general elections. After the 2001 AC elections, the IU-EB became members of the second Ibarretxe government in 2001. In the April 2005 AC elections, they gained three seats or 5.4% of the vote. The 2005 elections are discussed in further detail at the end of the chapter.

Figure 4.6: Number of IU-EB votes polled from 1986 to 2005

1986A:	12,000
1990A:	14,000
1991M:	17,000
1993G:	75,000
1994E:	86,000
1994A:	93,000
1995M:	81,000
1996G:	115,000
1998A:	70,000
2000G:	62,000
2001A:	78,000
2003M:	89,000
2005A:	3 seats (5.4%)

A =	for Autonomous Community assembly
E=	for European Parliament
G =	General elections (to Spanish *Cortes*)
M=	Municipal elections

EB and the Autonomic State

In the 14th congress of the *Partido Comunista de España* (Spanish Communist Party – PCE) in 1995, the leader Anguita faced a dual attack from the Catalans of the *Partit Socialista Unificat de Catalunya* (PSUC) led by Ribó and the *Comisiones Obreras* of Gutiérrez.[21] Anguita's line was against an alliance with the PSOE (which led to the distancing and later the exit of the *Nueva Izquierda* tendency), was in favour of the right to self-determination and was critical of the PCE's role in the transition to democracy. It was not viewed unkindly by the pro-nationalist tendencies within EB. For EB, IU's decisions to expel *Nueva Izquierda*, break with Ribó and denounce the *Esquerda Galega* coalition of socialists and local IU in Galicia, all of which took place in September 1997, were of no real concern. EB endorsed Anguita's defence of the unity of the peoples of Spain, to be furthered by the right to self-determination in a federal and republican state built on solidarity.

At the 5th IU assembly of December 1997, two thirds of the delegates backed Anguita, with one third against. This latter group also surfaced in EB, denouncing what it called the 'nationalist line' of the leadership, as seen in its questioning of whether EB should remain on the steering committee of the Ajuria–Enea Pact, of its support for the abortive ELA and LAB (Nationalist Trade Union Centres in *Euskadi*) demonstration against the imprisonment of the HB national executive in December 1997 and, above all, of its signing of the Lizarra declaration in September 1998.[22] The fall in the vote in the AC elections of October 1998 fuelled criticism from the anti-nationalist movement.

The struggle in the statewide IU between the Jacobin line of Frutos and the federalist line of Llamazares was resolved in the latter's favour when he was appointed leader. This suggests that Madrazo gained some breathing space within EB and was able to consolidate his position in favour of the right to self-determination for all the peoples of Spain, including the Basques, opting for a freely-chosen federalism within Spain. IU-EB's membership of the second Ibarretxe government in 2001, allowing Madrazo to become the caring face of the Basque government, helped the electoral position of EB which, as a member of the government, took on joint ownership of the Ibarretxe Plan from the start of its long journey in mid 2001.

However, as pressure from Spanish centralizers against the bill and against Basque nationalism per se intensified, branding any attempt to look critically at the concept of nationhood as 'betrayal of the nation', the pro-Basque choices made by EB became a major problem for the statewide party IU. Frutos' centralist group complained at Llamazares' support for Madrazo, blaming it for IU's failure to achieve electoral success across the whole of Spain. Perhaps because of this, and notwithstanding the fact that the whole of the Basque government is involved in the New Statute bill, IU-EB tabled a set of amendments, which had a bearing on nearly all the bill's articles, inspired by its own programme of freely chosen federalism in a federal Spain.

Herri Batasuna-Euskal Herritarok (HB-EH)

Historical Background and Party Ideology

Herri Batasuna (HB) was born as a coalition of left-wing nationalist parties in spring 1978, with two identifying markers. One was its opposition both to the Spanish constitution, which prevented the Basque people from exercising its right to self-determination, and to the Guernica Statute as a framework that fragmented the territorial unity of *Euskal Herria*;[23] the other, its support for ETA's political strategy. For twenty years until 1998 it was an anti-system party, ruled out of any governing coalition by its own choice and by the reality of the situation and subordinated to the clash between ETA and the police forces of the two governments, Spanish and Basque. A parallel structure, *Koordinadora Abertzale Sozialista* (KAS – Patriotic Socialist Committee) has taken decisions which are in fact directly connected to HB.

Electoral Performance and Party Structure and Leadership

HB's share of the vote, which rose slightly until the mid 1980s, coinciding with the crisis between the PNV and EA, has been falling slowly but steadily ever since. Its non-communication with the other parties in the system has increased since 1989–92, when there was the double breakdown of talks between ETA and the state (1989), and between the PNV and HB (1992).

HB stood in the last AC elections as *Euskal Herritarok* (EH). This indicates more than just a cautious attitude to the possibility of being declared illegal, and also the will to begin a process of transforming what had been a front of resistance, into a new national left-wing party. EH's results in the 1998 AC elections showed the existence of a pocket of at least one third of the voters who had previously abstained but now voted in favour of a Basque left that was non-violent.

Headed by Arnaldo Ortegi and Joseba Permach, the HB-EH leadership established firm relations with parties that had signed up to Lizarra, worked out an agreement to join Ibarretxe's government and became the main force behind *Udalbiltza*, a grouping of elected officials from parties from the Basque AC, Navarre and Iparralde which have all signed up to Lizarra. This group aims to forge links between the three parts of the Basque people beyond the administrative limits of Spain or the frontiers between Spain and France. However, EH accepted uncritically ETA's ending of the ceasefire in late 1999. After its dismissal from government, it boycotted the Basque parliament, weakening the nationalist majority, and proposed a process of constitutional unity for the three groups of the Basque people (the three provinces of the Basque AC, Navarre and Iparralde) that was unrealistic by any standards. In the general election of March 2000, it recommended abstention; in the AC elections of May 2001, its intransigence cost it 40 per cent of the vote it had won in 1998.

The process of re-founding HB as *Batasuna*, which culminated in spring 2001, led to the exit of the Aralar group, who disagreed on subjects ranging from the ending of the ETA ceasefire, to the withdrawal of EH from the Basque parliament, to the model of nation-building – which Aralar thought unviable and dismissive of Navarre and Iparralde. Aralar became a party in September 2001.

Figure 4.7: Number of HB-EH votes polled from 1986 to 2003

1986A:	199,000
1990A:	186,000
1991M:	172,000
1993G:	174,000
1994E:	140,000
1994A:	165,000
1995M:	160,000
1996G:	154,000
1998A:	222,000

2000G:	ABSTAINED
2001A:	142,000
2003M:	153,000 (votes for independents declared illegal)

A =	for Autonomous Community assembly
E =	for European Parliament
G =	General elections (to Spanish *Cortes*)
M=	Municipal elections

HB and the Autonomic State

The long drawn-out kidnapping by ETA of the businessmen Iglesias and Aldaia in 1993 and 1995 led to street fighting between pacifist groups demanding that the hostages be freed and supporters of radical nationalism. After a bad result in the 1994 European elections, there was an internal debate about the Oldartzen report, which recommended prioritizing nation-building, as opposed to waiting passively for ETA activities to bring results. During this debate a tendency critical of political violence emerged, supported by some 15 per cent of members. Its views preceded ETA's publication of its *Alternativa Democrática* (Democratic Alternative) in spring 1995, which replaced the previous line of negotiations between the state and ETA with another one, which in ETA's words would enable the citizens and the political and social forces of Euskal Herria (Basque People) to have their say. But the state was also required to recognize in advance the right to self-determination and the territorial unity of the Basque people. Such an unviable demand was bound to lead radical nationalism into conflict with the rest of the Basque political groupings and to 'spread the suffering across society'.

At the same time HB saw a dynamic alternative growing on the Basque left, in the form of *Elkarri*, which stressed a culture of dialogue. For three years, there was a two-way movement. On the one hand, some of HB attended the *Elkarri* peace conference of 1995, offered to talk with parties and trade unions about the Democratic Alternative and gave prominence to the video showing ETA's proposals for conflict resolution during their election campaigns. On the other hand, there was an extraordinary increase in tension between HB and the remaining Basque political and social groupings. Legal action against HB, in particular the arraignment of its national executive in early 1997, a piece of strong action that fitted in with what the PP government had been doing politically since 1996, did not unleash significant levels of solidarity or protest much beyond the MLNV and its immediate orbit. KAS, aware of this situation, released a document in December 1996 recommending 'political self-control', so as to reduce areas of tension in the relationships with other groupings. But such had been the tension created that this line was hard to put into practice, even if it did have the backing of the HB leadership.

The huge reaction to the murder of the PP councillor Blanco, a few months before the sentencing and imprisonment of the HB leadership, set off alarm bells among mainstream Basque nationalists, who feared the development of a situation that might weaken their ability to press for further development of statutory powers. The powerful reaction of HB activists to ETA's killing of the PP councillor Caso, which pulled the rug from under the protest demonstration called jointly by ELA and LAB, helped the new HB leadership elected in February to change tack, though this had been anticipated in a January document entitled *Línea de intervención política*. One figure filled the historic leadership vacuum in HB, Arnaldo Otegi, an ex-activist from ETA who had known prison and exile. The new leadership's support for democratic dialogue coincided with *Lehendakari* (head of the Basque government) Ardanza's proposal for an 'open-ended dialogue' to the steering committee of the Ajuria–Enea Pact. PNV and EA unease at the attitude of the statewide parties on the steering committee (PP and PSOE) to motions presented criticizing state terrorism went up a notch when they opposed Ardanza's suggestion. This would trigger the final crisis of the steering committee.

While the judiciary was shutting down the magazine *Egin*, a means of communication on the Basque left, discussions took place between parties favourably disposed to Basque self-government. These discussions began in February and March but went on for more than six months. The result was the Lizarra declaration of September 1998, signed by the following political parties: PNV, EA, HB and EB, as well as by the ELA and LAB unions and social movements like *Elkarri* or *Bakea Orain*.[24] The declaration which came out three days before ETA's unlimited ceasefire was supported by a majority of voters, as was very clear from the AC elections the following month.

Batasuna disapproved of the Ibarretxe Plan, accusing it of being too favourable to the system of ACs and perpetuating the division of the Basque people by concentrating solely on the territory of the Basque AC. The central government's offensive against radical nationalism, using all three powers – executive, legislative and judicial

– gave *Batasuna* back its identity markers. After the passage of the Law on Parties in spring 2002, the PP government and both houses of parliament, in a vote decided by the votes of the PP and PSOE (as all the peripheral parties and IU voted against or abstained), both requested the Supreme Court to begin the process of making *Batasuna* illegal, which was completed in March 2003. At the same time the High Court judge Garzón began a criminal lawsuit in September 2002 against the HB-Batasuna leaders of the past fifteen years, who were accused of belonging to an armed gang, while the party's meeting places, the *Herriko Tabernas*, were placed under judicial control by virtue of the same legal statute. The youth organizations of the radical nationalists, *Jarrai* and *Segi*, were accused of the same offence, as were the prisoner support groups, *Gestoras para la Amnistía* and *Askatasuna*. The radical nationalists called for protest demonstrations, which were also declared punishable on grounds of ETA membership. The central government forced the Basque government and its independent police force to break them up. On 14 September 2002, a crowd of some 50,000 people was dispersed by the *Ertzaintza* (Basque police), creating a new source of tension between radical and government nationalists. In March 2003, the Supreme Court ordered the Basque parliament to dissolve the *Socialista Abertzaleak* parliamentary group, which it refused to do in the name of parliamentary sovereignty, resulting in an unprecedented clash between different levels of authority within Spain.

Whilst they were prevented from standing in the municipal elections of May 2003, *Autodeterminazioraka Bilqunea* (AuB – Committee for Self-Determination) published a programme supporting self-determination, which led to hundreds of independent candidacies. The judiciary made AuB illegal, detained the municipal leaders of Udalbiltza and declared nearly all the candidacies null and void. Despite this, radical nationalism won some 150,000 votes in these elections, more than those won legally in the AC elections of May 2001. Aralar took 16,000 votes, half of them in Navarre.

After the tabling of the New Statute bill for the Basque Community, the discourse of radical nationalism shifted in tone. Head-on, unbending criticism gave way to something more nuanced. It was argued that the bill was important because it signified the demise of the Basque Statute and recognized concepts such as self-determination, which might hold a key to solving the conflict. However it was also argued that the bill was off the mark as it was firmly linked to the territory of the Basque AC. Radical nationalist initiatives were presented as being unchallenged and complementary to the bill and were seen as a means of putting pressure on the Ibarretxe Plan. Such was the spirit behind the setting up of a national forum for debate and Otegi's declaration of October 2003 in *El Pabellón Anaitasuna*. Radical nationalism still has to reach a resolved position on the final and credible abandonment of violence by ETA.

Basque Regional Elections April 2005

The PNV-EA won the regional elections but only by a small margin, losing their overall majority. PNV-EA won twenty-nine out of seventy-five seats (four less than in the previous elections). The PSOE came second with eighteen seats (an increase of five seats) and the PP third with fifteen seats (compared to nineteen in the previous elections). The Basque Communist Party (PCTV-EHAK) won an unprecedented nine seats, after the outlawed Batasuna had urged its supporters to back the PCTV. The PP called for the party to be declared illegal and their MPs prevented from taking up the nine seats they won.

With a minority government, Ibarretxe will have to rely on the PCTV votes to push his policies through the regional parliament. A closer alliance between the PSOE and the PNV-EA could be a possibility but the Ibarretxe Plan constitutes an obstacle to this.

Figure 4.8: AC Election Results – April 2005

PNV-EA:	29 out of 75 seats (38.6%)
PSOE:	18 out of 75 seats (22.6%)
PP:	15 out of 75 seats (17.3%)
PCTV-EHAK:	9 out of 75 seats (12.5%)
IU-EB:	3 out of 75 seats (5.4%)
Aralar:	1 out of 75 seats (2.3%)

Source: *Le Monde*, 19 April 2005

Conclusion

The Basque governments from 1980 to date have always included the PNV as the only or the dominant party. From 1980–5 the PNV formed single party governments. From 1985–7, a coalition programme was agreed between the PNV and the PSE. From 1987–98, the government was made up of a number of coalitions: PNV and PSE; PNV, EA and EE; PNV, PSE and EA. Since 1998 there has been a PNV-EA government with the IU-EB as a junior partner. This coalition has tended towards a sovereignist, pro-Basque line in its policies in opposition to the policies of the PP central government.

The political parties operating at the Basque Autonomous Community level can be characterized along different lines, but any such characterization must include an analysis of the parties' positions on Basque nationalism. In summary, the PNV is Basque nationalist and sought a third way between capitalism and socialism. The EA was created in 1986 out of a split in the PNV. This split was caused, amongst other things, by a difference of view on how the institutional model for the Basque Country should be structured. The EA held that such a model should be centralized, whilst the PNV held that it should be decentralized along the lines of the historic territories. The PSE-EE is the socialist party. Since the early 1980s the PSE has adopted the centralizing logic of its mother party, influenced by the continuing violence of ETA. The PSE-EE is distinguished from the PSOE in the fact that its subgroups differ in their stance towards Basque nationalism in the different territories. Their attitudes range from 'progressive' pro-nationalist to hard-line anti-nationalist. The history of the Basque PP is inextricably linked to Mayor Oreja and his opposition to Basque nationalism, although it seems as if this could be about to change. The UA was formed in 1990 out of a split from the PP over disagreements over the nationalist government's running of affairs in the Autonomous Community. The UA was therefore clearly forged in opposition to the Basque nationalist movement. However since the Lizarra agreement and as a result of the PP's increasingly strong stance against Basque nationalism, the UA has become increasingly irrelevant as a party. The IU-EB is strongly linked to the Spanish IU. The pro-Basque decisions made by the EB have increasingly become a problem for the statewide IU, which has put pressure on IU-EB to take a more centralist stance. HB-EH started out as a pro-Basque nationalist anti-system party (which supported ETA's political strategy). However since the signing of the Lizarra agreement, the HB-EH leadership has established firm relations with the parties who signed up to that agreement.

However it is the tabling of the New Statute bill for the Basque Autonomous Community which has resulted in a shift in tone in the debate on radical Basque nationalism. It is argued that whilst the bill has its flaws, it at least recognizes the concept of self-determination. It inspired the setting up of a National Forum for debate on the question of radical nationalism. However, radical nationalism still has to reach a unified position on the final abandonment of violence by ETA.

The relatively small margin of victory for the PNV-EA in the April 2005 Basque regional elections can be interpreted as a blow to the Ibarretxe Plan for increased autonomy for the Basque region (which had already been rejected by the Spanish parliament in February 2005). The elections were a test of the Basque population's support of the Plan, with Ibarretxe making it clear that a vote for the PNV-EA in the regional elections would in effect be an endorsement of the plan. The equivocal election results for the PNV-EA therefore represent a further setback to the plan.

Notes

[1] See J. Cara Baroja, *Los Vascos* (Minotauro, Madrid, 1958).

[2] See Daniel-Louis Seiler, *L'exemplarité du nationalisme basque: une perspective comparée* (Fundación Sabino Arana, Iruña, 1996).

[3] See Francisco Letamendia, "Basque nationalism and the struggle for self-determination in the Basque Country" in B. Berberoglu (ed.) *The National Question* (Temple University Press, Philadelphia, 1995).

[4] This is understandable given the high percentage of Catalans who speak Catalan and the ease with which a Castilian immigrant can understand and learn the language, while Basque is much less accessible. An excellent comparison of the two nations may be found in Daniele Conversi, *The Basques, The Catalans and Spain: Alternative Routes to Nationalist Mobilisation* (Hurst & Co., London, 1997).

[5] The upper bourgeoisie and the Spanish military stationed in the Basque Country supported Franco.

[6] This needs to be qualified by stating that many Basque nationalists and even members of ETA and HB are also from this group of immigrants.

[7] The foral laws give the Basque Country and Navarre a great deal of financial autonomy. The Foral Deputation, not the Spanish state, first collects taxes of various kinds. These are then divided according to a complex formula between those which remain in the AC and those which go to the central state.

[8] The sentiment on the part of richer regions that they are subsidizing the poorer is not confined to the Basque Country and may be found in Catalonia but also in Italy's northern regions such as Lombardy.

[9] See Joseba Zulaika, *Basque violence. Metaphor and Sacrament* (Nevada University Press, Reno, 1988).

[10] They have been responsible for over 800 deaths and many bombings in different parts of Spain.

[11] See Francisco Letamendia, *Juego de espejos, Conflictos nacionales centro-periferia* (Ed. Trotta, Madrid, 1997).

[12] Richard Gillespie, 'Peace moves in the Basque Country', *Journal of Southern Europe and the Balkans,* Vol. 1, no. 2, 1999, pp. 119–36.

[13] The concept of *parti de cadres* was invented by the French political scientist Duverger to describe the smaller, parliamentary-based groups of loosely organized politicians, usually moderates or conservatives, which preceded modern mass organizations with an extensive membership, such as socialist or communist parties.

[14] The Concierto is a financial agreement between central government and the AC government which sets out financial contributions from both over a ten-year period. See J. Loughlin and S. Martin, *op cit.*

[15] Elkarri is an environmentalist movement close to the radical wing of Basque nationalism. It was able through these contacts to keep in touch with the radicals, while at the same time getting closer to Gesto por la Paz, a peace organization close to the PNV. Together, these organizations sought to bring all the main actors to the negotiating table, without the exclusion of radicalism implied in the Ajuria–Enea Pact. Elkarri sponsored a peace conference in 1995, but with disappointing results.

[16] Iparralde is the northern part of the Basque country, currently located in France (mostly in the département of Pyrénées-Atlantiques). The province of Navarra is also claimed by Basque nationalists as a constituent part of Euskadi, along with the territory of the existing Basque AC. Navarre has different political traditions, however, and its political élites stress their own specificity as well as their Basque background.

[17] The Plan provided for such features of national sovereignty as a Basque ID card, direct representation of the Basque country in EU institutions, a Basque Supreme Court and the possibility for Basque governments to hold referenda. There was clearly no way that it could ever be approved by the *Cortes.*

[18] Party premises which had educational, cultural and entertainment functions as well as party-political ones. An approximate Welsh equivalent would be the Miners' Institutes.

[19] The Grupos Antiterroristas de Liberacion were unofficial death squads, of a type familiar in Central or South America, which assassinated over 25 alleged terrorists in the 1980s; journalistic revelations in the 1990s suggested a degree of cover for their operations at the highest levels of the state. FILESA was a consultancy agency involved in channelling illegal funds to the Socialist Party.

[20] Constitutional patriotism is a concept borrowed from the German sociologist Jürgen Habermas, who argued from a left-wing position in favour of a reasoned, dispassionate loyalty towards public institutions on the part of citizens; it implies a critical distance from the more emotional commitment that underlies much of modern nationalism. In PP discourse, however, it has tended to mean un-questioning loyalty to the status quo as interpreted by the PP, particularly on the question of the possible evolution of the ACs, which in this view should be frozen forever in the 1978 arrangements. Anyone disagreeing with this is by implication unpatriotic.

[21] The CC.OO. are trade unions founded clandestinely during the Franco dictatorship and politically close to the Spanish Communist Party.

[22] ELA (often known as ELA-STV Solidaridad de Trabajadores Vascos, or Basque Workers' Solidarity) and LAB (Laugile Abertzalean Batzordeak, or Nationalist Workers' Union) are the main nationalist trade union centres in Euskadi, the latter being closer to the radical wing of nationalism.

[23] That is, it blocked any possibility of the three parts of the historic Basque territory ever being united in a single political entity.

[24] In Spanish, Paz Ahora (Peace Now) – a pacifist organization.

5

Nationalist Parties in Galicia

M<small>ICHAEL</small> K<small>EATING</small>

Historical Background: Political Traditions in Galicia

Galicia, in north-western Spain, is one of the three 'historic nationalities', with its own culture and language and a tradition of nationalist politics. Compared with Catalonia and the Basque Country, however, nationalist parties have been extremely fragmented, divided by issues of regionalism vs nationalism, left vs right, Catholics vs secularists, social democrats vs Marxists, pro-Europeans vs anti-Europeans and all manner of personal and factional differences. In recent years, however, nationalism has been consolidated into a united front, the *Bloque Nacionalista Galego* (BNG) which, while still a federation rather than a single party, has managed to establish a more coherent image, was for a time the second political force of Galicia and in 2005 entered into the governing coalition with the socialists.

Galicia is somewhat isolated from the rest of Spain, looking rather to the maritime Atlantic world. Geographically, linguistically and culturally it is nearer to Portugal, but separated from it until recent years by the national border, although now the European single market has generated much cross-border cooperation. Galicia is divided between a maritime economy on the coast, with a large fishing fleet, and an agrarian interior characterized by a very dispersed settlement pattern. Population is dispersed across the region, agricultural holdings are divided into very small plots (*minifundia*), and communication among the towns and villages has always been rather poor. There is a tradition of large-scale emigration, both to the other parts of Spain and to Latin America. In these circumstances, political mobilization has proved difficult and politics has developed within clientelistic networks. In the nineteenth century, these focused on local notables, known as *caciques*, who controlled the distribution of government patronage and resources, in return for social and political support in the localities. Since the transition to democracy, these client networks have been taken over by the political parties.

A prominent mark of identity in Galicia is the language, which is closely related to Portuguese. Galicia is, in fact, the historic nationality within the Spanish state in which the local language is most widely known, with over 95 per cent of the population able to understand, and over 90 per cent to speak it. This has a lot to do with the lack of immigration from other parts of Spain, unlike in Catalonia and the Basque Country where expanding industries brought in workers from outside. Galego, however, has not enjoyed the prestige and status of Catalan or Basque, being widely regarded as a peasant language, so that the urban bourgeoisie and the middle class professionals tend to use Castilian. Modernization and progress have been equated with integration into Spanish culture, while Galician culture is often portrayed as inherently traditionalist and even backward. This has posed a formidable obstacle to the development of a progressive and modernizing nationalism on Catalan lines, which might link the defence of culture to self-government, economic dynamism and engagement in the new Europe.[1]

There was, as in other peripheries of Europe, a cultural revival in the late nineteenth century, a central theme of which was a myth of Celtic origins developed and promoted by Murguía.[2] It is true that Galicia has many affinities with other Celtic nations like Ireland[3] not only in landscape and climate but in music, ancient burial rituals and oral folk traditions, although there is no Celtic influence in the language. The cultural revival gave rise in the past to a regionalist political movement seeking a degree of autonomy within Spain. During the First World War, under the influence of events elsewhere in Europe, regionalism gave way to a more explicit nationalism under the *Irmandades da Fala*, in which Galicia was portrayed as a stateless nation with its own history and traditions. The movement was suppressed under the dictatorship of Primo de Rivera in the 1920s but reappeared under the Second Republic from 1931, notably in the form of the *Partido Galeguista* of Castelao. Like the earlier regionalisms, the new Galician nationalism was divided between conservatives and progressives, traditionalists and modernizers and the party picture was highly fragmented. A statute of autonomy parallel to those of Catalonia and the Basque Country was negotiated and passed in a referendum but it never came into effect because Galicia fell under the control of the right-wing insurgents at the beginning of the Civil War – Franco himself was a Galician. The nationalist movement was then divided between a group in exile, initially led by Castelao, and an internal group which focused on cultural matters rather than directly political issues.

The Transition to Democracy in 1978

With the transition to democracy after 1978, a new statute of autonomy was negotiated and put to a referendum. There was little opposition, but little mobilization either and the statute was passed overwhelmingly but on a turnout of just 29 per cent. In the first autonomous elections, the turnout was just 46 per cent, but the figure has shown a steady tendency to increase since then, as the autonomous institutions of Galicia have established themselves and become rooted in society.[4] The party system has remained highly fragmented, especially on the nationalist side, although recent years have seen a trend to consolidation and a three-way pattern of competition among the conservative, socialist and nationalist options.

Fig 5.1: Turnout in Galician elections, 1981–2005

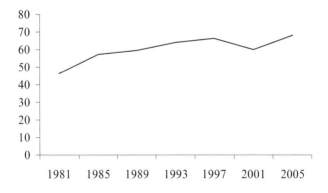

Party Politics in Galicia

Politics in the early years of the Galician autonomous government were unstable, with the only consistent formation being the local branch of the Spanish Socialist Party, PSOE. From the late 1980s, however, politics has been dominated by the Popular Party (PP), led by Manuel Fraga Iribarne, one of the most remarkable personalities in Spanish politics. A minister in the Franco regime, Fraga was regarded as a relative 'liberal' and a modernizer and, after the transition, formed his own party which eventually adopted the name *Partido Popular*. While this became the national opposition to the socialist government elected in 1982, Fraga could never quite shake off his Francoist image and was widely regarded as unelectable at the national level. In 1989 therefore he moved back to his native Galicia and, assuming the leadership of the local PP, gained an absolute majority in the Galician parliament, which he retained until June 2005. The system created by Fraga during the long period of his leadership in Galicia is an essential key to understanding Galician politics. An erstwhile centralist, he quickly adopted the theme of a conservative Galician regionalism, which he carefully distinguishes from nationalism. This allowed him to incorporate the more conservative elements of the regionalist tradition and its support base.[5] In 1998 the PP even tried to appropriate the memory of Castelao, organizing an act of homage at his birthplace on the 48th anniversary of his death, much to the chagrin of the nationalist opposition.[6] While the socialists were in power in the central government (1982–1996) he was able to play the Galician card to complain about centralization, neglect and bad policies on the part of Madrid. He also practises a contemporary form of the old *caciquismo*, with extensive clientelistic networks across the region. Each of the four provinces of Galicia is run by a PP *baron*, who distributes patronage through the town and village mayors, and, when the PP was in power, controlled a number of the ministries in the regional government. Within the Galician PP there are diverse factions, including a traditional and regionalist one, a Spanish centralizing one, and a more modern neo-liberal one inspired by developments outside, all brought together under Fraga's powerful personality. Fraga's standing has allowed him to pursue a range of initiatives, notably on the Europe of the Regions, without fear of reprisals from Madrid. He was an indefatigable traveller, maintaining a friendship with Fidel Castro and daring even to visit Gadaffi in Libya. It remains to be seen, after his defeat in the June 2005 elections, whether the new governing coalition will modify this system.

Nationalist Politics in Galicia

Nationalism re-emerged in Galicia after the transition, but in a typically fragmented way. It would be too confusing to try and relate the whole evolution[7] but essentially the various formations have been defined by their position on the right-left spectrum and on the regionalist–nationalist one. The most important effort at a centre-right nationalism was the *Coalición Galega* (CG) descended from the historic *Partido Galeguista*, and which was also involved in the *Operación Roca*, the effort launched from Catalonia to establish a Spanish liberal party. CG benefited from the collapse of the statewide *Unión de Centro Democrático* of Adolfo Suárez, which took down its Galician branch with it. Between 1987 and 1989 CG participated in a short-lived coalition government in Galicia with the socialists but with the arrival of Fraga and his broad appeal, it went into rapid decline. A series of parties on the moderate left, notably the PSG, also failed to advance significantly and folded into other formations. This left the far left, which was able to dominate nationalism for a number of years ensuring that, in a largely conservative society, it would remain a marginal force. Again, there is a bewildering set of names and initials. The oldest organization is the *Unión do Povo Galego* (UPG) founded in 1964 as a hard-line Marxist-Leninist party decidated to the national liberation of Galicia. This formed the core of the *Bloque Nacional Popular Galego* (BNPG) which in 1982 became the *Bloque Nacionalista Galego* (BNG). Gradually absorbing the other nationalist formations, the BNG has, since the late 1980s, gradually become the dominant force in Galician nationalism, under the charismatic leadership of Xose Manuel Beiras. It benefited immeasurably from the decline of the Socialist Party (PSOE) in Galicia, which was regarded as too oriented towards Madrid and suffered from a series of internal crises from the late 1990s. At the same time, the BNG has absorbed most of the other elements of Galician nationalism, from the liberals of the old CG, through the social democrats, to the far left.

The BNG is now a complex formation, with both direct membership and affiliation through parties, each of which accounts for about half the total. It includes *Unión do Povo Galego* and *Colectivo Inzar* (communist in origin); *Colectivo Socialista, Esquerda Nacionalista* and *Unidade Galega* (social democratic); *Partido Nacionalista Galego* (centre-left); and various smaller groups. There are 23 territorial branches based on *comarcas*, each with its own council. The supreme authority is the National Assembly, which meets every two years and at which all members can speak and vote. A National Council consists of a representative from each *comarca* and two from each affiliated party, plus twenty-five members elected on a proportional basis from lists at the National Assembly. A national spokesperson (*portavoz*) is elected from the National Council. In spite of the egalitarian sound of this title, Beiras was long accepted as the undisputed leader of the BNG.

Figure 5.2 shows how the BNG rose steadily from the late 1980s to displace other nationalist formations, overtake the socialists, and become the official opposition to the PP in 1997. Since then it has been racked by internal opposition, culminating in the departure of Beiras, and has declined to the benefit of the socialists. In 2001 the two parties were equal in votes and seats but in 2005, benefiting from the popularity of the relatively new Spanish socialist government of José Luís Rodriguez Zapatero, the Galician socialists moved ahead.

Figure 5.2: Percentage vote in autonomous elections, Galicia, 1991–2005

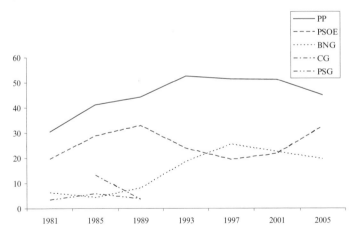

Figure 5.3 shows the distribution of seats in the Galician parliament, where the PP has held an absolute majority since 1989 and fragment-ation has given way to a three-party division.

Figure 5.3: Seats in the Galician parliament, 1981–2005

	1981	1985	1989	1993	1997	2001	2005
PP	26	34	38	43	41	41	37
PSOE	16	22	28	19	15	17	25
BNG	3	1	5	13	19	17	13
UCD	24						
Other parties	1	14	4				

Advances in the autonomous elections were matched by success at other levels. At the Spanish elections of 2000, the BNG gained 306,000 votes, compared with 220,000 in 1996. Its municipal vote increased from 208,000 in 1995 to 290,000 in 1999. Most dramatically of all, its vote in the European elections soared from 131,000 in 1994 to 332,000 in 1999. In addition to its presence in the Galician parliament, the BNG has, in 2005, two deputies in the Spanish parliament, one senator and nineteen local mayors. Between 1999 and 2004 it had a Member of the European Parliament but in the latter year, competing as part of the Galeusca formation with Basque and Catalan nationalists, it failed to elect a member.

The rise of the BNG can be explained partly by social change and the crisis in the Socialist Party in the late 1990s. Above all, however, its success is due to its evolution from a hard-line leftist and fundamentalist nationalist party, into a broad based party of territorial defence.

Ideological Repositioning

Ideologically, the BNG, in the form of UPG, started as a Marxist-Leninist party and this marked its positions in the early years. Its intransigent nationalism was illustrated in 1984 when two of its three members in the Galician parliament were expelled for refusing to swear to the Spanish constitution. Xose Manuel Beiras, the only member elected in 1985[8] is an academic economist from a strongly left-wing background, the author of a famous book, *O atraso económico de Galicia*, which traced Galicia's economic backwardness to its social and political structure.[9] The party took a strongly anti-European stance in the 1980s, seeing the EC as a capitalist club which would merely exacerbate the disadvantages and peripherality of Galicia. Its ideology was based on the concept of Galicia as an internal colony and the need for radical change. Solidarity was expressed with other stateless nations of Europe, but with a special emphasis on the Basque National Liberation Movement (this is a term for the movement around ETA as distinct from the moderate Basque Nationalist Party).[10] From the mid-1980s, however, it started to position itself as a mainstream party. In 1987 it expelled the PCLN, an extreme faction supporting political violence, and in 1989 it brought in *Esquerda Nacionalista* and *Unidade Galega*, formed from the social democratic nationalists, along other democratic leftist forces like the movement *Inzar*.

The BNG insists that this was a tactical move in order to establish a needed presence in the institutions, rather than a major ideological shift. Indeed, the ideological repositioning took a little longer as the BNG stuck with a rather populist line, retaining strong elements of the old anti-colonialist rhetoric. The BNG's basic beliefs, laid out in the early 1980s and repeated in party papers through the 1990s, were as follows:

- Galicia is a nation with the right to self-determination;
- democracy is the fundamental principle;
- democracy requires opposition to monopolies and the defence of popular interests;
- self-management is the principle of national organization, through the parties, trade unions and mass organizations;
- Galicia is colonized;
- anti-imperialism requires that Galicia oppose NATO and the European Community;
- world peace and disarmament are essential;
- Galicia needs a new social model breaking with colonial dependence. This will involve controlling its own financial resources for investment at home; local control or nationalization of strategic resources; nationalization of energy and natural resources and their extraction; development of agriculture and fishing; industrialization to create a non-dependent economy; specific policies for sectors in crisis because of world conditions and Spanish government policy; reform of urban planning; a free universal health service; free, secular and coeducational schools; normalization of Galego as the language of Galicia.

This was accompanied by a rather demagogic line and opportunistic opposition to the effects of economic restructuring and a defence of all sectors in decline.

By the late 1990s, however, as the BNG became the official opposition, advanced to control more municipal councils and became a contender for power in the autonomous government, the rhetoric was softened and detailed policies began to emerge. Its 1997 programme for the autonomous elections contained a detailed list of policies soberly argued, without any reference to colonialism. Instead of nationalization, there was a reference to the need for the Galician administration to be present selectively in the economy in the form of public enterprise or public–private partnerships, without prejudice to the need to maintain a competitive market economy. This allowed it to extend its support base and pose as a credible alternative to the PP, while still tapping the discontents provoked in Galicia by economic restructuring and the crises in the agricultural, fishing and extractive sectors.

The BNG's line on nationalism has also softened somewhat. They were never quite clear about the nature of the national self-government they sought, but the early rhetoric was quite radical, couched in anti-colonial terms and embracing the language of the Basque radicals. This, along with their left-wing opinions, distanced them from the more conservative nationalists of CiU in Catalonia and the PNV in the Basque Country. In the late 1990s, however, they drew closer to CiU and PNV to argue the need for a new approach to the nationalities question in Spain on the basis of the idea, developed by the Catalans, of a plurinational state. This would lead eventually to an asymmetrical confederation of nations (Spain, Catalonia, Galicia and the Basque Country); in the meantime there should be recognition of the status of the historic nations as different from the other autonomous communities. The proposal was incorporated in the 1998 Declaration of Barcelona, followed by Declarations of Bilbao and Santiago de Compostela. This was a quintessentially Catalan approach to the nationalities question in Spain and papered over a lot of differences among the three parties. It stalled when the PNV sought to launch a peace process in the Basque Country by forming a nationalist front with *Herri Batasuna-Euskal Herritarok*, while CiU was drawn into governing pacts with the PP both in Madrid and Barcelona. Nonetheless, the declarations did mark a step forward for the BNG, putting it on the same level as the other two parties and helping it to gain credibility in Spain as a whole. It also drew attention to the material benefits that Catalans and Basques gained from investing in support for nationalist parties, which had held the balance of power in two Spanish elections, in 1993 and 1996. The BNG, recast as a party of territorial defence, could now offer to perform the same role for Galicia at some future time.

The BNG's elusive stance on the long-term constitutional future of Galicia puts it in the company of many minority nationalist movements in Europe, which are moving beyond classic conceptions of the sovereign nation state towards a post-sovereign order. So they abjure both autonomy within Spain and separatism, arguing that Galicia, as a nation, has the right to self-determination but that this might be exercised in a variety of different constitutional frameworks. As European integration advances, more opportunities will be opened for stateless nations and, in the meantime, the future should not be prejudiced by accepting the rigid constitutional frameworks of today. In the meantime, the movement prefers to focus on concrete economic and social issues, arguing that these need to be addressed in a distinctively Galician way.

So the BNG's programme for the autonomous elections of 1997 referred to the model of the confederal or plurinational state and called for the transfer of more competences, especially in economic matters. It demanded the application in the long run of the Basque *concierto económico*, in which the autonomous government would raise most taxes and pass on a proportion to Madrid. In the short term it called for a transfer of income and value added taxes. Yet, conscious of the weak economic position of Galicia they continued to press for inter-territorial solidarity in Spain and Europe, even while pressing, as a medium term objective, for the full fiscal sovereignty of Galicia.[11] The programme laid heavy stress on economic development, which took up more than half of its 187 pages. Education, language and culture formed the other main concern, with thirty-seven pages. Social, heath and labour policies get twenty pages, with the remainder devoted to women, the environment, local government and social exclusion. There was nothing on independence and very little on constitutional issues generally.

In 2004, the BNG, like the other nationalist parties in Spain, drew up more precise proposals for the constitutional status of Galicia. This drew on the topical theme of the plurinational state, accepting the Spanish framework while calling for more powers, a set of bilateral institutions to regulate relations with the state, and participation in the European Union as part of the Spanish presence.[12] This looked like a realistic basis for negotiation with the socialist Spanish government in the context of simultaneous negotiations in Catalonia and other autonomous communities.

Attitudes towards Europe have also modified over time. In the early years, the European Community was condemned as a capitalist and imperialist operation against the interests of the Galician people. This allowed the BNG to capitalize on the serious problems of adaptation of the Galician economy and on the crisis in the fishing industry, which could be blamed on the Common Fisheries Policy. In 1988–9 there was a debate over whether the BNG should present candidates for the European parliament, given its fundamental opposition to the institution. Eventually it was decided that absenting themselves would be irresponsible and called for unity around a single candidate to represent Galicia. In fact, since Spain comprises a single electoral constituency for European elections, they had to present a whole list, in the hope that Galicians would plump for it in sufficient numbers to get their top candidate elected. Their programme called for a minimal reform, which would give each nation (including Galicia) direct representation with a right to veto any Community action that was against its interests. For the 1994 European elections, the BNG list was headed by Carlos Mella, a moderate who had been a minister in the brief coalition government of 1987–9 with the socialists (and which had not included BNG). In 1999, they again presented a whole list of 64 candidates and this time one was elected. In 2004 the BNG joined with nationalists in Catalonia and the Basque Country to present the Galeusca list (Galicia–Euskadi–Catalonia) but did not elect a member.

The evolution of attitudes can be seen in comparing the declarations of the 1995 National Assembly with those of 1998. In 1995, the BNG declared that it was clear that the integration of Galicia into a supranational institution by the adhesion of Spain to the EU had led to the destruction of its weak productive structures, of its incipient centres of decision making and of hardships unimaginable ten or fifteen years previously. It condemned the Maastricht Treaty and affirmed its 'opposition to the European Union, hegemonized by big multinational capital'.[13] By 1998 it had accepted that the EU was an inescapable reality and that Galicia needed to be present wherever possible in its institutions.[14] There was support for a more social Europe and concern about the democratic deficit, but the focus was on improving the EU and not destroying it. In the long term, the BNG dreams of replacing the state-based EU with a Europe of the Peoples ɔut recognizes that this will require a lengthy evolution and that in the meantime there are interests within Europe that the BNG must defend, including securing a good share of Structural Fund and agricultural spending. This more positive attitude paid handsome dividends with a 77 per cent increase in its vote for the European elections from 1994 to 1999.

The nationalists and their supporters

The leadership of the BNG is overwhelmingly middle class and professional. Of their eighteen members elected in 1997, fourteen were university graduates. Six were teachers, three of them at university level, two were lawyers and two architects. There appear to be no manual workers or farmers, in spite of the BNG's working class orientation, although two had come up through the nationalist trade union. A key factor in the movement's success was certainly the charismatic leadership of Xosé Manuel Beiras, a shaggy-bearded intellectual active since the 1960s, who is never seen wearing a tie. Beiras is a fiery orator able to combine demagogic oratory with sharp academic analysis and has appeal well beyond his home territory on the far left.

Figure 5.4: Percentage vote by province, 2005

	A Coruña	Ourense	Lugo	Pontevedra
PP	42.5	50.7	49.1	43.8
BNG	21.5	17.5	15.2	20.1
PSOE	32.5	30.0	33.7	33.0

Geographically, the BNG does better in the coastal and more industrial provinces of A Coruña and Pontevedra than in the interior rural areas of Ourense and Lugo, still dominated by the PP machine. In the large cities of Santiago de Compostela, Vigo, and A Coruña, the nationalists scored well, as they did in the medium-sized towns of Pontevedra and Ourense. Surveys indicate that its support base is quite diverse, but with a special appeal to young voters and urban professionals (Pallarés, 1998). It also has strong links to the trade union world, with its leading role in the main Galician union, the *Confederación Intersindical Galega*, which has a clear nationalist stance, and the agricultural unions. It is well organized in comparison with most Spanish parties, with an active membership base. In some small communities it has become the dominant force, picking up over 70 per cent of the vote. The BNG has benefited greatly from the problems of the Galician socialists. Socialists in the Basque Country or Catalonia can follow a twin strategy. They draw on the support of immigrant workers from the rest of Spain, and they are able to project a moderately Basque or Catalan image to the indigenous working class. The Galician socialists have no immigrant working class, and have failed to project themselves as a soft nationalist alternative to the BNG, while being outflanked on regionalism by the PP. Given the salience of regionalism in Spanish politics generally and the utility of having strong regionalist parties to bargain for powers and resources, this has left them vulnerable. It has also prevented them taking up the cultural aspects of Galician nationalism. As if their image of being a *sucursalista*, or 'branch plant' party were not enough, the socialists were damaged by a series of internal factional and personality conflicts in the late 1990s. So it is no surprise that the BNG did well in the cities and other natural socialist strongholds.

The 1999 municipal elections represented a major step forward for the BNG's strategy of implanting itself in the institutions. Faced with their own weakness and the dominance of the PP, the socialists agreed to form coalitions with the nationalists in several municipalities. As a result, the BNG saw fifteen of its candidates elected as mayors, including in the important cities of Ferrol, Pontevedra and Vigo – where they were helped by a split in the PP, which had kicked its incumbent mayor upstairs to a place on the list for the European elections. In 2003, their haul was increased to nineteen mayors. This municipal presence not only provides a platform for the BNG to air views, it also gives it control of resources to distribute to its supporters in the form of substantial rewards. In Galician politics, this is a vital source of political influence and electoral gains.

Conclusions: Future Prospects

Given the structure of their vote, the long term prospects for the nationalists appear promising. They appeal to the young and upwardly mobile and are strong in the expanding regions of the coast and the cities, leaving the declining countryside to the PP. Their ideological evolution into a party of territorial defence, with a strong emphasis on economic and social issues, allows them to make further headway against the socialists. The very heterogeneity of the BNG permits it to appeal to voters of all social classes and, having outpaced the socialists, to make inroads into the PP support base. On the other hand, the BNG has also relied on charismatic leadership, in the form of Xosé Manuel Beiras who, like Fraga, is able to hold together parts of a rather disparate movement. His withdrawal was followed by a loss of votes to a Socialist Party that is now able to appeal to the same social groups.

There is a growing market for regionalism in Galicia, as citizens identify more with their autonomous institutions, trust them more than the central government, and look to the parties to defend their territorial interests in Madrid and Brussels. Support for centralized government fell from 29 per cent in 1970 to 6 per cent in 1990.[15] The market for nationalism, however, remains smaller than in Catalonia and the Basque Country. A 1996 survey found that just 16 per cent of the people in Galicia considered their region to be a nation, compared with 34 per cent in Catalonia and 40 per cent in the Basque Country.[16] Other surveys have shown that Galicians are contented with the degree of autonomy they have and are much less willing than Catalans and Basques to go further.[17] Support for self-determination or independence languishes around two per cent, compared with figures between 20 and 30 per cent in the other two historic nationalities. A 1996 survey showed just 21 per cent of Galicians in favour of a federal or con-federal state, compared with 50 per cent in Catalonia and 63 per cent in the Basque Country (independence was not an option here).[18] This would suggest that a condition for nationalist advance is a further moderation of the message, away from fundamentalist nationalism and towards a regionalist discourse with a strong cultural dimension, embedded in a European framework. The following years saw such a moderation. At the same time, the Socialist Party across Spain adopted a more accommodating attitude towards the nationalities following the accession to the leadership of José Luis Rodríguez Zapatero and his arrival in power in 2004. In the same year, the Catalan socialists formed a coalition with Esquerra Republicana de Catalunya to dislodge Convergència i Unió from office. This was part of the political climate in which, following Fraga's failure to gain an absolute majority at the Galician elections of June 2005, the socialists were able to form a coalition with the BNG. So, despite their losing support since the late 1990s, the nationalists were able to enter government. Their moderated nationalism was able to meet the socialists, themselves moving in a more autonomist direction, to discuss the possibilities of renewed autonomy within a changed Spain.

Notes

[1] Michael Keating. 'Rethinking the Region. Culture, Institutions and Economic Development in Catalonia and Galicia', *European Urban and Regional Studies*, 8.3 (2001), 217–34.

[2] Ramón Máiz, '*Nación de Breogán*: Oportunidades políticas y estrategias enmarcadoras en el movimiento nacionalista gallego (1886–1996)', *Estudios Políticos*, 92 (1996), 33–75.

[3] Elizabeth Keating, *Afinidades culturais entre Galicia e Irlanda* (Galaxia Vigo, 1988).

[4] Ramón Máiz and Antón Losada, 'Institutions, Policies and Nation Building: The Galician Case', *Regional and Federal Studies*, 10.1 (2000), 62–91.

[5] Ramón Máiz, '*Nación de Breogán*: Oportunidades políticas y estrategias enmarcadoras en el movimiento nacionalista gallego (1886–1996)', *Estudios Políticos*, 92 (1996), 33–75.

[6] El Correo Gallego, 7 January 1998

[7] There is a good account in Ramón Máiz, '*Nación de Breogán*: Oportunidades políticas y estrategias enmarcadoras en el movimiento nacionalista gallego (1886–1996)', *Estudios Políticos*, 92 (1996), 33–75.

[8] The party passed a special resolution allowing him to take his seat even though he had to submit to the 'anti-democratic and fascist' practice of swearing to the Spanish constitution and the Galician statute of autonomy.

[9] Xosé Manuel Beiras, *O atraso económico de Galicia* (3rd edn.) (Laiovento, Santiago de Compostela, 1995).

[10] Bloque Nacionalista Galego, *Ponencias aprobadas en la III Asemblea Nacional do BNG celebrada no Carballiño*, 7–8 February 1987.

[11] In fact these two demands are in the same paragraph. Bloque Nacionalista Galego, *Programa de Governo, Autonómicas '97*, Santiago de Compostela, 1997, p. 22.

[12] Bloque Nacionalista Galego, *Documento de bases para a elaboracion dun novo estatuto para Galiza*, 2004.

[13] Bloque Nacionalista Galego, *VII Asemblea Nacional, En bloque por Galiza. Ponéncias asembleárias*, Ferrol, December 1995, p. 16.

[14] Bloque Nacionalista Galego, *VIII Asemblea Nacional, Galiz sairá gañanda. Con intelixeéncia e ilusion. Ponéncias asembleárias*, Ourense, June, 1998.

[15] Manuel García Ferrando, Eduardo López-Aranguren and Miguel Beltrán, *La conciencia nacional y regional en la España de las autonomías* (Centro de Investigaciones *Sociológicas*, Madrid, 1994).

[16] Féliz Moral, *Identidad regional y nacionalismo en el Estado de las Autonomías*. Opiniones y Actitudes 18 (Centro de Investigaciones *Sociológicas*, Madrid, 1998).

[17] Manuel García Ferrando, Eduardo López-Aranguren and Miguel Beltrán, *La conciencia nacional y regional en la España de las autonomías* (Centro de Investigaciones *Sociológicas*, Madrid, 1994).

[18] Féliz Moral, *Identidad regional y nacionalismo en el Estado de las Autonomías. Opiniones y Actitudes 18* (Centro de Investigaciones *Sociológicas*, Madrid, 1998).

6

Spanish Political Parties outside Spain

David Hanley

Like their counterparts in other countries, Spain's political parties play an active role in the two main transnational arenas where parties come together, namely party Internationals and the European Union, in which the European Parliament (EP) plays a modest but increasing role in the decision-making process of the Union.

The main party families from all countries have long associated in Internationals, the first such organizations dating back to the latter half of the nineteenth century, with the socialists leading the way but soon followed by the Christian democrats and liberals. These bodies, which operate worldwide, allow national parties from the same political family to bring their leaders together to discuss issues, hammer out ideas and programmes, help emergence of young parties in new democracies and sometimes vet the credentials of parties seeking to use the family label or arbitrate between rival claimants to the label. Internationals are especially useful when parties are out of government and looking for a new profile. The Internationals are not, and never have been, some embryonic form of global political government, but they do perform a very effective task of low to medium level co-ordination. In recent years, some Spanish parties have developed quite a high profile at this international level.

Aznar's *Partido Popular* (PP), in particular, has invested much effort in the Christian Democrat International (CDI), seeking in particular closer contacts with Central and South America, where Christian democrat parties have some weight. This fits well with longstanding Spanish foreign policy interests, which have sought to develop privileged relations with Latin America. He has helped the CDI move away from traditional Christian democracy towards the model of a less

specific centre-right organization, in which Christian Democracy be-
comes simply one element (and arguably an increasingly less important
one) among various conservative, liberal or centre-right parties, who
have in common mainly their opposition to social democracy and their
desire to gather strength through numbers.

The PP's influence can be seen in gestures such as the CDI's acceptance
into membership of the Argentine *Partido Justicialista*, better known
as the Peronists, a vast nebula in which the handful of Christian democrats
are far outnumbered by conservatives, populists, worshippers of the
free market and adepts of old-fashioned clientelism. The weight of the PP
within the CDI is reflected by the latter's change of name in November
2001 to Christian Democrat/Centrist and Democrat International
and the election of Aznar as president. It is often the case with such
international organizations that national parties make use of them so
as to present their leader as a statesman of high international profile.
This has been the case for Aznar, whose ambitions at the level of the
European Union have frequently been the subject of speculation.

The *Partido Socialista Obrero Español* (PSOE) has also had a close
relationship with the Socialist International (SI). The party's sustenance
in exile and its recovery after the transition to democracy owed much
to the SI and particularly the financial support of the German Social
Democratic Party (SPD) and its Ebert Foundation. The socialists'
first leader after the transition, Felipe González, when in office, also
used the SI to strengthen links with Spanish-speaking socialists and
to reinforce his image beyond Spain. Today he is a much-respected
elder statesman of the SI.

As for the European Union, it would be hard to overestimate PP
influence in recent years. The party had secured membership of the
parliamentary group of the European People's Party (EPP), as the
Christian democrats in the EP are known, even before Aznar's election.
Their admission was regarded as a crucial test for the identity of the
EPP. Hitherto it had been dominated by classic Christian democrats,
especially the Italian *Democrazia Cristiana* (DC) and the Christian
democrat parties of the Benelux countries. These parties stood for a
less market-oriented type of society and economy, with a strong welfare
state, based on the concepts of the 'common good' and of the 'person',
understood as a co-operative rather than a competitive being and who
had multiple identities in his or her community, nation, or religion.
This explains the strongly pro-European integration attitudes of
Christian democrats and their dislike of nationalistic politics. All this

puts classic Christian democracy at some distance from Anglo-Saxon types of conservatism, as represented by Margaret Thatcher for example. However, the German Christian Democratic Union-Christian Socialist Union (CDU-CSU), the biggest party within this federation of national parties that was the EPP, wanted to open out the group to conservative forces in general, even at the risk of diluting the Christian identity of the EPP. This was with the aim of making the EPP the biggest group in the European Parliament (EP), ahead of the socialists. Impending enlargement of the EU to take in Scandinavian countries, where there is no Christian democrat tradition, made the widening of the party imperative from the German viewpoint. The PP was thus a sort of Trojan horse, basically a conservative party with a few Christian Democrat trimmings. The collapse of the Italian party system and in particular of the DC in the early 1990s gave the expansionists their chance. The PP got into the group and later into the party.[1] Once the breach was opened, the PP was followed by Berlusconi's *Forza Italia* and other non-Christian Democrat parties like the liberal Portuguese *Partido Social Democrata* (PSD). Even the British Conservative Party would have been a full party member by now (instead of merely a member of the parliamentary group) had it been able to pay a few words of lip-service to the federalist aims of the EPP charter. Thus far, this has proved too much for it. The result of all this is that the EPP has become a broad centre-right organization, rather like the PP within Spain. This is reflected in the renaming of the parliamentary group, which is now EPP-ED, the ED standing for European Democrats. Spanish influence within EPP has been recognized by the election of Alejandro Agag Longo as secretary general (replaced by Antonio López Istúriz when he resigned to concentrate on his business interests soon after marrying Aznar's younger daughter). Control of the parliamentary group, as opposed to the party, remains within German hands, however, which may say something about which is the more important of the two organizations.

The great rival of the EPP is the PES (Party of European Socialists), and here the PSOE has played a key role, as befits a party which has always made up one of the biggest national delegations within the socialist group. Enrique Barón Crespo was president of the EP after 1989 and chairs the PES parliamentary group today, and another PSOE leader to make his mark in Brussels was Manuel Marín at the Commission. Former party leader Josep Borrell is president of the EP for the first half of its term until the end of 2006.

Smaller Spanish parties are also active in the smaller EP groups and the Transnational Parties (TNPs) which gravitate around the big two, EPP and PES. One consequence of the PP's joining the EPP was the departure of the Basque *Partido Nacionalista Vasco* (PNV), a party with much more claim to a classic Christian democrat profile (see chapter 4 of this book) than the PP. Numbers count in parliamentary arithmetic, however, and once the PP was let in, the only place for the single PNV deputy was elsewhere. In recent years, its member has usually sat with the European Free Alliance (EFA), the group of regionalist parties allied to the Greens in the European Parliament. The EFA has now become a fully-fledged party known as the DPPE-EFA, the first acronym standing for Democratic Party of the Peoples of Europe. The PNV recently had observer status within the EFA, where at times it must have felt uncomfortable among the radical politics espoused by many of the parties in this group. José Luis Linazasoro of EA has proved a very able coordinator for the EFA group, however. By way of contrast, it is interesting to note that the Catalan *Unió Democràtica* has retained membership of the EPP alongside the PP (as a rule only one party per country tends to be allowed membership of the big TNPs, and the PP could undoubtedly have elbowed the Catalans out had it so wished). Its failure to do so no doubt reflects the greater weight of Catalonia within statewide politics in Spain and the need to keep Catalan politicians on board, particularly when the majority margin in Madrid may be tight.[2]

Smaller Spanish parties which are members of the EFA include *Unitat Catalana* and *Esquerra Republicana* from Catalonia, the Basque *Eusko Alkartasuna*, the *Bloque Nacionalista Galego* and the *Partido Andalucista*. Not all of them have MEPs elected. Nationalist MEPs from the Canary Islands have also sat in the group. Recent requests for observer status in EFA-DPPE have been filed by the *Partit Socialista de Mallorca-Entesa Nacionalista* and the *Bloc Nacionalista Valencià*. All of this bears testimony to the continuing vigour of regionalist parties within Spain and their desire to coordinate activity with like-minded parties across Europe.[3]

Finally the post-communists of the *Izquierda Unida* (IU) have usually been members of the leftist group in the EP now usually known by its French initials GUE (*Gauche Unitaire Européenne*). Currently it has one MEP out of approximately forty belonging to this group, compared with four in the last EP. The GUE defends fairly traditional notions of socialism, as opposed to those of 'modernizers' and advocates of a 'third way'. In late 2004, the GUE launched a fully-fledged TNP known in English as the PEL (Party of the European Left). IU signed up as a full member, along with the rump of the old communist party PCE and the small Catalan *Esquerra Unida i Alternativa*.

Conclusion

The EP elections of 2004 revealed more about internal Spanish politics than they did about Spain's relationship to the EU; but this is true of almost all states, given that voters tend to see these contests as mere 'second order' elections, where very little decision-making power is at stake. Thus voters can protest with impunity and lash out against incumbent governments. This the Spanish voters did, though most of the anger was still directed at the recently defeated PP rather than at the new socialist government.

Of the 54 Spanish seats, the PSOE took 25, against 24 for the PP (the 1999 figures were 24 and 27 respectively out of a total of 64). The smaller parties were badly squeezed. In 1999 they took 13 seats out of 64, but this time only 5 out of 54. Two of these went to a moderate nationalist list grouping the BNG, CiU and PNV, and a third to a more radical nationalist list combining the Catalan ERC, Basque EA and Aragonese nationalists. A joint IU and Greens list shared the remaining two. The MEPs elected for the big battalions of the PSOE and PP sat with the PES and EPP as before, but some adjustment took place among the smaller parties. The IU representative continued in the leftist GUE, and his Green colleague went to the Green group, but the remaining nationalists parted company, the radical MEP joining the Greens/Regionalists and the two moderate nationalists ending up in the expanded liberal group, which seems increasingly to be a home for disgruntled federalists from other political families.[4]

These elections show the dominance of the statewide parties in Spain, but they also demonstrate that the smaller nationalist parties can, by having joint lists, punch somewhere around their true weight. The EP certainly gives them and similar parties from other large states another arena in which to voice their distinct message.

This brief survey of party activity outside Spain demonstrates the relevance across the whole of Europe of the cleavages that produced the Spanish parties. In particular, the conflict between centralizers and regionalist/subnational forces remains sharp, and the European Parliament is simply one arena among many where it surfaces again.[5]

Notes

[1]   It is important to distinguish in the European Parliament between party groups of MEPs and the transnational parties (TNP). The groups, formed along the lines of traditional party families, predate even the creation of the European Economic Community in 1958, having their origins in previous bodies such as the Coal and Steel Community. They have always been the mechanism through which national parties coordinated the action of their MEPs with those of similar family inside the EP. Since the EP has been elected directly (from 1979) the national parties have formed transnational federations which during 1990 became actual TNPs. Up till now the groups have had the lion's share of cash, staff and other resources. The recent adoption of the Party Statute by the EP should in theory make the TNP less dependent on the groups, but it remains to be seen whether the TNP will actually become more influential.

[2]   Dowling, A. (2004) 'Convergència i Unió, Catalonia and the new Catalanism' in S. Balfour (ed.) *Politics in Contemporary Spain*, London, Routledge, 106–19.

[3]   On regionalist party activity in the EU see Dewinter, L. and Tursan, H. (eds) (1998) *Regionalist Parties in Western Europe*, London, Routledge; P. Lynch (1996) *Minority Nationalism and European Integration*, Cardiff, University of Wales Press.

[4]   Typical refugees from the EPP include the followers of the Italian Romano Prodi and the UDF of the Frenchman François Bayrou. These MEPs are Christian Democrats by origin who have become tired of the increasingly lukewarm federalism of the EPP and see the Liberal group as the only federalist option, despite having differences with a family of rationalist and secularist origins. The PNV which has now gone into the Liberal group fits very much into this pattern.

[5]   For an introduction to TNP, which sets Spanish parties in a European context, see D. Bell and C. Lord (eds) (1998) *Transnational Parties in the European Union*, Aldershot, Ashgate; J. Gaffney (ed) *Political Parties and the European Union*, London, Routledge; S. Hix and C. Lord (1997) *Political Parties in the European Union*, Basingstoke, Macmillan; A. Kreppel (2002) *The European Parliament and the Supranational Party System: a Study in Institutional Development*, Cambridge, Cambridge University Press.

Appendix I

Chronological History of Spain

2nd century BC	Arrival of Romans: Spain part of Roman Empire.
306 AD	Council of Elvira: Spanish Catholic Bishops meet.
8th to 15th centuries	Moorish Spain.
910–1230	The Kingdom of Galicia goes through various periods of self-rule and rule by Leon and/or Castile before definitively becoming part of Castile.
1137	Dynastic union of the county of Catalonia with the kingdom of Aragon.
1469	The kingdom of Aragon/county of Catalonia is linked to Castile through the marriage of Ferdinand and Isabella.
1492	Reconquista of Spain from the Moors by the Catholic Monarchs, Ferdinand and Isabella.
1512–16	The kingdom of Navarre becomes part of the kingdom of Aragon and then Castile.
1516	Carlos I accedes to the throne as the first ruler of a united Spain.
16th century	Spain, under Carlos I and Felipe II, most powerful country in Europe.
1701–1714	The War of the Spanish Succession.
Early 19th century	Napoleonic Occupation and War of Independence (1808–1814).
19th century	Wars between liberals and Carlists, loss of colonies.
1873–1874	First Republic.
1874	Restoration of the monarchy.
1931	The Second Republic.
1936–1939	Spanish Civil War.
1939–1975	Francoist dictatorship.
1959	Creation of ETA.

1975	Death of Franco; Juan Carlos sworn in as king.
1976	Legalization of political parties.
1977	General elections, centre-right coalition UDC largest party, Suárez prime minister.
	Spain becomes a member of the Council of Europe.
1978	Approval of new democratic constitution defining Spain as a parliamentary monarchy.
1979	General elections, second victory of UCD.
1980	Catalonia and Basque Country become first Autonomous Communities.
1981	Attempted *coup d'état* by group of Civil Guards.
1982	Socialists win an absolute majority in general elections and Felipe González becomes prime minister.
	Spain becomes a member of NATO.
1986	Spain joins EEC.
	General election: PSOE maintains its position as majority party.
1989	José María Aznar becomes leader of Popular Party. PSOE wins general elections for third successive time but majority reduced to one seat.
1993	Fourth PSOE victory in general elections but rules as a minority government dependent on Basque and Catalan nationalists.
1996	General elections: PP emerges as largest party but dependent on minority parties.
2000	General elections, PP retains its dominance in elections and is no longer dependent on minority parties.
2004	11 March – al Qaida explode bombs in Madrid, killing more than 200 and wounding 1,000, just before general elections.
	14 March – general elections lost by Aznar and PP because of mishandling of bombing incident, PSOE, led by Zapatero, take over government.

Source: T. Lawlor, M. Rigby et al., *Contemporary Spain* (London: Longman, 1998) and miscellaneous other sources.

Appendix II

Spanish Political Parties: An Overview

N.B. Some of the parties in this list are early or later versions of others, e.g. the AP mutated into the PP. For details, see the various chapters.

Statewide Parties

Right
AP   Alianza Popular (People's Alliance)
CDS   Centro Democrático y Social (Social and Democratic Centre)
PP   Partido Popular (People's Party)
UCD   Unión de Centro Democrático (Union of the Democratic Centre)

Left
IU   Izquierda Unida (United Left)
PCE   Partido Comunista de España (Spanish Communist Party)
PSOE   Partido Socialista Obrero Español (Spanish Socialist Workers' Party)
V   Los Verdes (The Greens)

Regionalist/nationalist Parties

* Parties marked thus can be considered as the regional branches of statewide parties

BNG   Bloque Nacionalista Galego (Galician Nationalist Coalition)
BNV   Bloc Nacionalista Valencià (Nationalist Coalition for Valencia)
CDC   Convergència Democràtica de Catalunya (Democratic Convergence of Catalonia, with UDC)
CiU   Convergència i Unió (Convergence and Union) [Catalonia]
EA   Eusko Alkartasuna (Basque Solidarity)

ERC	Esquerra Republicana de Catalunya (Catalan Republican Left)
HB-EH	Herri Batasuna-Euskal Herritarok (Popular Unity-Basque Unity)
*IC-V	Iniciativa Els Verds (Green Initiative) [Catalonia]
*IU-EB	Izquierda Unida-Ezker Batua (United Left-Basque Left)
PA	Partido Aragonés
PNV	Partido Nacionalista Vasco (Basque Nationalist Party)
*PPC	Partido Popular de Catalunya (People's Party of Catalonia)
*PSC-PSOE	Partit dels Socialistes de Catalunya (Party of Catalan Socialists)
*PSE-EE	Partido Socialista de Euskadi-Euskadiko Ezkerra (Basque Socialist Party-Basque Left)
PSM-EN	Partit Socialista de Mallorca-Entesa Nacionalista (Majorcan Socialist Party-Nationalist Alliance)
*PSUC	Partit Socialista Unificat de Catalunya (United Catalan Socialist Party)
UA	Unidad Alavesa (Alava Unity) [Alava Province, Basque Country]
UDC	Unió Democràtica de Catalunya (with CDC)

Appendix III

The Spanish Electoral System

The Spanish legislature the *Cortes Generales* consists of two chambers: a lower house, the *Congreso de los Diputados* or Congress of Deputies, and an upper house, the *Senado* or Senate. The lower house, or Congress, has 350 members who are elected by universal adult suffrage for four years. The constituencies coincide with the fifty provinces, each of which has a minimum of two seats in the Congress of Deputies, plus one additional seat for every 144,500 inhabitants or fraction over 70,000 inhabitants. The North African cities of Ceuta and Melilla each have one seat. Elections to the Congress of Deputies use the d'Hondt, or largest average, system of proportional representation (PR) while elections to the Senate adopt a majority system. To qualify for election a party must obtain a minimum of 3 per cent of the vote. Four Senate seats are allotted to each province whatever their population. The cities of Ceuta and Melilla use the plurality or first-past-the-post system (the same one as used in the United Kingdom).

All adults aged 18 and over are eligible to vote. Voting is done by party list. The lists contain the same number of names as there are seats in the constituency and are closed and fixed, which means that once the lists are registered, they cannot be changed.

The d'Hondt electoral system

The highest average system divides each party's votes by successive divisors and then allocates seats to the parties in descending order of the quotients.

Four-member constituency, 20,000 votes cast division by d'Hondt divisors

Party	Votes	Divisor: 1	Divisor: 2	Divisor: 3	Total Seats
A	8,200	8,200(1)	4,100(3)	2,733	2
B	6,100	6,100(2)	3,050(4)	2,033	2
C	3,000	3,000	1,500	1,000	0
D	2,700	2,700	1,350	900	0
TOTAL	20,000				4

Source: Dick Leonard and Richard Natkiel, *World Atlas of Elections: Voting Patterns in 39 Democracies*, The Economist Publications, London, 1986, p. 3. quoted in Brian O'Neal, "Electoral systems", Library of Canadian Parliament, May 1993.

In this example, the number of votes received by each party is successively divided by d'Hondt divisors (1, 2, 3). Seats are allocated once the use of all the divisors has been completed; in this way it is possible to compare the quotients and allocate the seats on the basis of their descending order. Party A, with the highest quotient of 8,200, is awarded the first seat; its third-highest quotient of 4,100 gives it the third seat as well. Party B's second highest quotient of 6,100 gives it the second seat and its quotient of 3,050 gives it the fourth, and last, seat. It is clear from this example that the d'Hondt system tends to award seats to parties that receive the largest share of the votes cast, a factor which indicates that this system does not provide a large measure of proportionality.

Index

["